THE BEST IN MAGIC

THE BEST IN MAGIC
BRUCE ELLIOTT

ILLUSTRATED BY LOUIS RAVIELLI

GALAHAD BOOKS • NEW YORK CITY

Contents

♥ ♣ ♦ ♠

Contents

Preface

♥ ♣ ♦ ♠

In the Foreword to my first book, *Magic as a Hobby*, Orson Welles made this point: "It is entirely possible that this excellent book should never have been published . . . not for general sale."

His reasoning was that since magic is dependent on mystery, any book or explanation serving to pull aside the curtain of mystery does a disservice to magic in general.

In the golden days of vaudeville this point would have been well taken, for when the goateed greats like Herrmann and Kellar were performing in every town, big and small, magic was brought directly to the people, and a person enchanted by it soon discovered ways of learning how to become a magician.

But today, with vaudeville dead, with stage shows no longer touring, (Blackstone is the last of the old-time magicians to perform a full evening show), with too little magic being shown on television—it seems to me that the new magician must come from the ranks of those who read books like this one. Otherwise magic is certain to become a dead art.

Since I love magic dearly I would not like to see it fade away, behind other hobbies.

The majority of magic books written for the beginner cover a series of tricks that have become so hackneyed the interested amateur soon finds little to stir his interest, no matter how many such books he buys.

Preface

I have attempted in these pages, with the aid of many friends who have contributed thousands of tricks to my magic publication, *The Phoenix*, to bring to the interested amateur new, easy tricks that require no expensive apparatus, and which in the main require little or no skill.

There are effects in this book that *do* require skill, and they are some of the best tricks I know. I have included them because I know that, for magic to prosper, the beginner must have a challenge. No hobby is satisfying that caters always to the unskilled. But no matter what your sphere of interest, these pages are packed with effects that will amply repay study.

In the words of one of the wisest magicians I have ever known, the late Dr. Jacob Daley, "The great tricks are those combining a maximum of effect with a minimum of manipulative hazard."

This is the yardstick I have applied to the tricks you will find described here. I hope you will get as much pleasure from reading them as I have had in assembling them for you.

Bruce Elliott

" 'Tis magicke, magicke that hath ravisht me. . . .'"
Dr. Faustus

—CHRISTOPHER MARLOWE

CHAPTER I

♥ ♣ ♦ ♠

Novel Effects All Designed
for Close-Up Performing

Dearest to my heart of all magic is that dubbed "micromagie" by our European friends, but which Americans call close-up magic. Both terms tell a little. The foreign term implies smallness; the American the fact that these tricks are designed to be done not on stage, but literally under the spectators' noses—small magic done with small props at close range. This, to me, is the ideal kind of prestidigitation.

Because of the restrictions as to size and working conditions, magic performed in this manner has a most startling effect to the beholder.

This chapter will concern itself with such tricks—and will employ for magic purposes such unlikely objects as an auto distributor cap, paper clips, a purse frame, a spoon, and some thimbles.

JIM-DANDY VANISHER [*Jim Shannon*] *

This device can be made for a dime. Despite the fantastic effects possible with it, all that is involved is a rubber distributor cap that can be bought at an auto supply store for a nickel (Fig. 1). If you fasten the cap to a length of elastic, fasten the elastic up your sleeve or around your middle (which is a better place), running the elastic through your belt loops and fastening

* Bracketed names after titles of tricks are those of the originators.

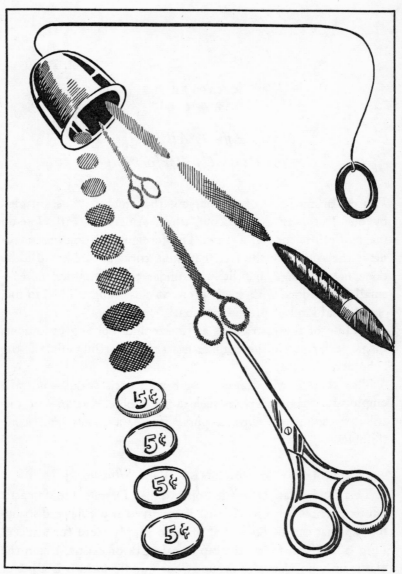

Fig. 1

the far end of the elastic to the back of the top of your trousers with a safety pin, you are all set for a series of astonishing effects with a simple device.

Because the distributor cap is made of soft but tough rubber, it will clasp firmly such diverse objects as loose coins, a scissors, or a cigar.

A good first trick with the gadget entails holding five pennies in one hand with the distributor cap on top of the coins. Borrow a nickel, press down with your thumb on the perimeter of the cap, flattening it enough so that the nickel will be forced into it. Let the cap be pulled under your open jacket—by the stretched elastic which whirls it out of sight—then allow the hidden pennies to drop into sight.

While the spectator looks at the pennies, reach under your coat and recapture the rubber cap. Holding it in your left hand pressed down by your thumb against the palm of your hand, pick up the pennies one by one and press them into the vanisher alongside the nickel that is already there.

Later, having emptied the coins out of the rubber cap, push the round loop of the handle of a pair of scissors into the rubber cap, and let go. The scissors whip under your coat and out of sight.

I know of no gadget as simply made that has so many uses. Make one up and try it for the vanishing or changing of any objects which will allow themselves to be jammed into the tough rubber cap.

POP-OFF [*W. Bowman*]

Here is one of the latest close-up novelties to delight magicians.

Required are two ordinary paper clips and a borrowed dollar bill.

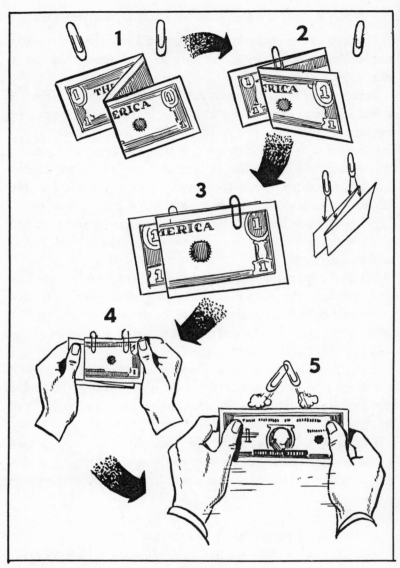

Fig. 2

The clips are placed separately on a folded dollar bill, The magician pulls on the ends of the dollar bill and the two paper clips pop off the bill and drop to the table linked! (See Fig. 2.)

Fold the bill as shown in #1. Place the first paper clip on the bill as in #2. The second paper clip is placed as in #3. The inset drawing to the right of #3 shows the proper placement of the clips.

Hold the dollar bill as in #4. Pull outward on the ends of the bill (#5) and the pulling action will make the paper clips pop off the bill and link simultaneously.

A TWIST THROUGH THE WRIST [*John Boyko*]

Two paper clips, a piece of string, and five minutes of practice make up this startling, impromptu penetration effect. It is based on a rope-through-lady trick invented by "Gen" Grant.

The string, about 28 inches long, is knotted at the ends to form a loop. Slip two paper clips on the loop (Fig. 3). Hold a clip in each hand as in #1, making sure the *double wire* end of each clip points upward as shown.

Bring the hands together, grasping both clips with the right thumb, as pictured in #2. The clips should be held by the extreme upper finger tips, making them invisible when the hand is viewed from above.

Ask the spectator to raise his right arm "like this," illustrating the action by extending your left arm forward, palm up. This provides a reason for taking both clips momentarily in the right hand.

While the spectator is preoccupied with extending his arm properly, your left hand seizes the cord below clip A, as in #3. Separate your hands, simultaneously carrying the string beneath the spectator's wrist as in #4. The action should look as though you took a clip in the left hand. Both hands appear the same to

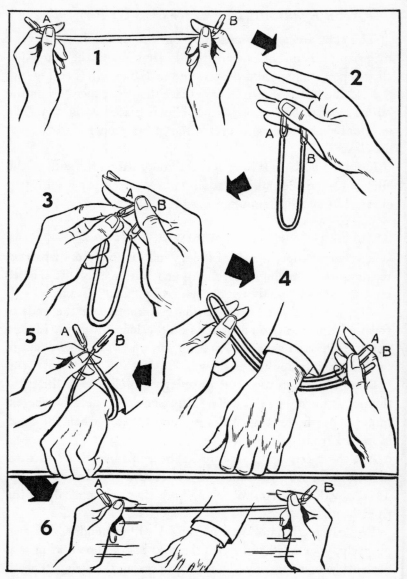

Fig. 3

the spectator (if he should happen to look down at them), which is why the clips in the right hand must not be visible from above.

Immediately bring your hands together above his wrist, seizing the lower end of both clips with your left thumb and forefinger. The right hand fans the clips in a "V" formation (#5) and moves away.

The cord appears to be looped around the wrist, with a clip at each end. Actually, both clips are on one end, with the left fingers holding the free end of the loop in place.

Grasp the clip on your right with the right hand, your left hand retaining its hold on the left clip. Move the hands apart quickly. The clip in your left hand will slide along the cord. As the cord pulls straight, it gives the illusion of penetrating the wrist (#6). All now can be examined.

NICKEL-PLATED [*Derek Vernon*]

One of the greatest of all table stunts is the one where you seem to bend a spoon or a fork in half. Jay Marshall added the touch where you lock your pinky under the spoon so that you can lift the "bent" spoon off the table. The drawings in Fig. 4 show this locking move.

The next step is the addition of a coin, a nickel, to the effect. The small bit of the curve of a nickel showing above the hand, as in Fig. 4, #1, will imitate perfectly the top of almost any silver-plated spoon.

This means that after you apparently have bent the spoon, as shown in the illustrations, the bit of coin showing above the hand gives the last bit of illusion to the bent spoon trick.

Hold the nickel as in Fig. 4, #1. The correct finger position is shown in #2. A side view of the situation (#3) shows why the onlookers are convinced you have really bent the spoon.

7

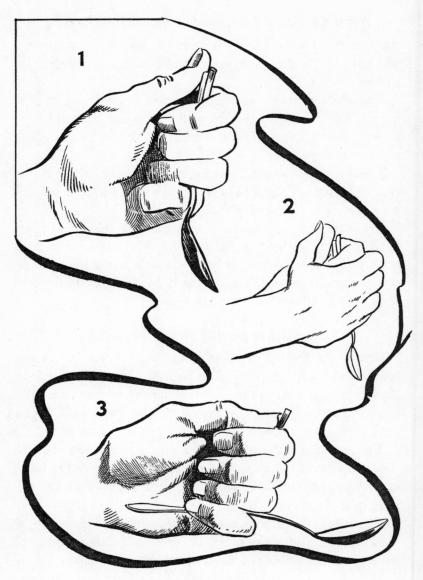

Fig. 4

Allow as little of the coin to show as possible, and do not comment on it. Your audience will see it.

Get rid of the coin after you have dropped the spoon back on the table. The audience will be so surprised at seeing the spoon unbent that you will have no trouble in dropping the coin in your pocket.

PURSE [*Bill Nord*]

Show the metal frame of a little purse. That is, cut off the leather or cloth which ordinarily makes the pocket of the purse and retain just the metal hinged top (Fig. 5.) Showing this— and your hand—to be innocently empty, open the clasp and insert your thumb and forefinger into the open frame. From the "invisible" purse you draw out a completely real handkerchief.

This is very pretty visible magic. Besides the little metal frame you need the silk handkerchief—a small one—and two thumb tips, one of the metal type, the other rubber. Put the rubber thumb tip on top of the metal one. Push the silk into the thumb tip.

The loaded thumb tip is on your right thumb, the metal frame of the purse is in your left hand held between the very tips of the thumb and middle finger. The metal frame is closed.

With the thumb and middle finger of the right hand, flip open the metal frame and insert the thumb and middle finger into the opening of the purse as you would if you were reaching into a real purse. The thumb tip is pressed in between the fore and middle fingers of the left hand down at their bases. They grip the tip, allowing you to pull the silk out of the tip up into view.

Under cover of the expanding silk, and once the silk is out of the thumb tip, reinsert your thumb into it, getting rid of the

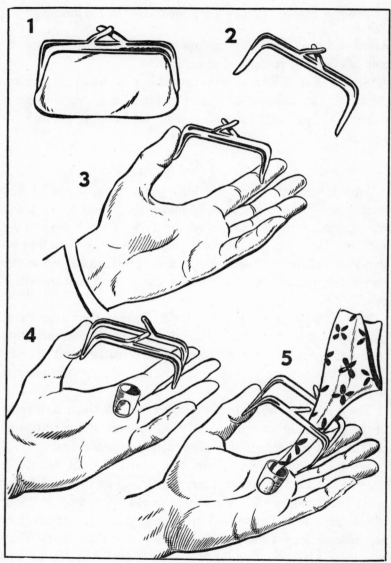

Fig. 5

evidence. Your hands are seemingly empty and you have produced a silk from nowhere.

The reason for the rubber thumb tip on top of the metal one is to deaden the click the metal tip would make in opening the frame. The reason for the inner metal tip is twofold. It allows you to grip the tip more firmly (there is a danger that the rubber one will close in on itself), and the metal lining allows the silk to come out more readily.

Your patter story can be about the purse itself which you pretend is cloth-covered. Your attitude is that there is nothing surprising in what you are doing, it is only to the spectators that the cloth of the purse is invisible.

The purse looks like #1 when you buy it. Illustration #2 shows it after you have discarded the cloth or leather. The way the frame looks in your left hand when you display it is shown in #3. Sketch #4 shows the inside of your hand, which the spectators do not see, after you have loaded in the thumb tip. The right hand is omitted for the sake of clarity.

RISE [*H. G. Frank*]

A little white ball about three-quarters of an inch in diameter with a one-eighth inch hole drilled through it is needed, as is a four-inch length of plastic drinking straw. In the course of the effect a ball is slid over a straw, and the straw held as shown in Fig. 6, #1. Slowly the ball creeps up the straw and then back toward the thumb. The hand can be shifted to the positions indicated by #2 and #3. The ball continues to rise and fall slowly. A nice effect can be had by moving the hands from one side of the body to the other. As the hands are moved from side to side, they should pivot around the tip of the thumbs.

The working mechanism is a thin black thread. It should be approximately eighteen inches long. One end is fastened to the

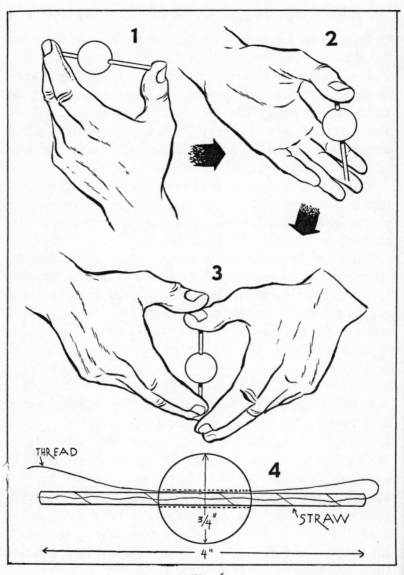

THREAD

1

2

3

4

3/4"

STRAW

4"

Fig. 6

belt strap on the left hip. The other end is fed into the straw. A small plug of wax should be put in each end of the straw. This will prevent the thread from sliding out when the straw is carried in the pocket (#4.) After allowing the ball to rise and fall in the various positions, have it answer questions by bobbing up and down.

At the end of the routine the straw is simply pushed forward toward one of the spectators, the thread slips out unnoticed and falls against the left leg. A trial will prove how mysterious the illusion is.

It is important that there are no rough edges at the end of the hole for the thread to catch on and unravel.

Although the method used is not new, the presentation *is* different.

REUNION [*Don Tanner*]

Simple, easy, convincing methods of accomplishing effects are most desirable, since under these circumstances all of the performer's efforts may be directed towards presentation.

A cigarette, after being freely displayed, is cut through the center. The two halves are displayed separately, placed together and "magically" restored into a whole cigarette.

The cigarette used is a prepared one. It is half again as long as a regular cigarette. The special cigarette is prepared by placing three cigarettes end to end and rolling them in a piece of tissue paper or onion skin paper and then sealing this "extra" wrapper with glue. A cigarette three times as long as a regular cigarette is the result. If this is then cut through the center with a razor blade, the result is two prepared cigarettes, each one being half again as long as a regular cigarette.

The cigarette package must now be prepared. This is done by making a small hole in the bottom of the package. The hole should

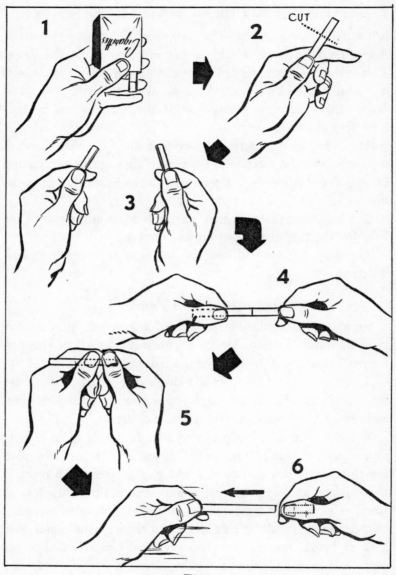

Fig. 7

be just *slightly* smaller than the diameter of a cigarette. One of the prepared cigarettes is then placed in the package, its extra length protruding from the hole in the bottom (Fig. 7, #1). Since the hole is slightly smaller than the cigarette, it will keep the cigarette from falling out. The prepared cigarette and package are carried in the pocket.

Remove the pack from the pocket, concealing the protrusion with the fingers of the hand as shown in #1. Remove the prepared cigarette from the pack, concealing its extra length with the hand (#2). It will appear that you are holding the cigarette by its end. With a pair of sharp scissors cut the cigarette through the "center" (actually, where the half joins the whole) indicated by the dotted line (#2). Pick up the piece cut off and display (apparently) half of the cigarette in each hand (#3). Now place the two pieces together (#4). Slide the fingers along the cigarette (#5). Apparently slide the fingers back again, although actually the fingers of the right hand stay where they are and the fingers of the left hand slide back to the end of the cigarette (#6). Carry the cigarette away to the left, displaying it apparently restored. The short piece left in the finger palm position of the right hand is disposed of in the pocket as you reach for a book of matches to light the cigarette.

VARIANT [*John P. Hamilton*]

Here is a variation of a standard thimble penetration. I like it because there are no fake looking moves about it and, if you could actually make a thimble penetrate a handkerchief, this is the way it would look.

Needed is one red thimble, and an eighteen-inch blue silk handkerchief. Display the thimble as shown in Fig. 8, #1, on the index finger of your right hand. With your left hand grasp the silk along one of its borders as in #2. Drape the silk over

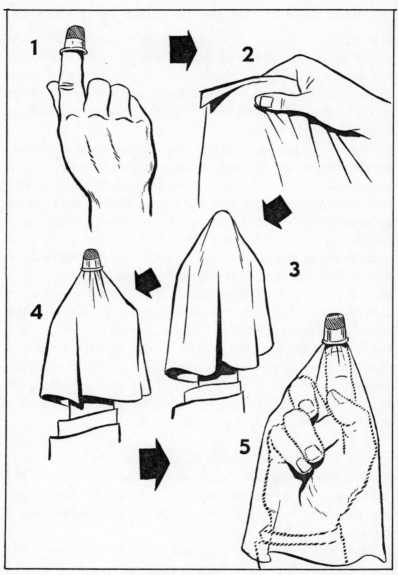

Fig. 8

your right hand (#3). As you cover your right hand with the silk, your index finger bends down and places the thimble into the thumb palm and immediately straightens up again as the silk covers it. Now your middle finger takes the thumb-palmed thimble onto itself.

It is now necessary to grasp a little of the handkerchief in the crotch of the right thumb and arrange it so that, although your entire hand seems to be covered from the front, the fingers at the rear are free with the exception of your index finger (#5).

To accomplish the penetration, lower your right hand a few inches and then thrust it upwards. On the upward thrust your middle finger with the thimble on it straightens out behind your index finger as in #5. Viewed from the front this creates a perfect illusion, as though the thimble popped up through the silk on your index finger (#4).

With the thumb and forefinger of the left hand lift the thimble slightly and place it on the right index finger, which is beneath the silk. As you do this, bend your right hand forward and down, letting the silk fall downward, and continue to hold your left index finger on top of the thimble. Then let the silk fall back over your right hand and the thimble is truly on your index finger and over the silk.

To the spectator it appears that the thimble penetrated the silk. Then, to display it better, lower your right hand and as you lower it put your index finger on the thimble to prevent it from falling off.

A silk handkerchief works better than a cotton one, since it flares out around the top of your index finger, thereby better concealing your middle finger in back of it.

ANOTHER RISE [*Carlo Rossetti*]

Fig. 9, #1, shows a thimble on the forefinger of the right

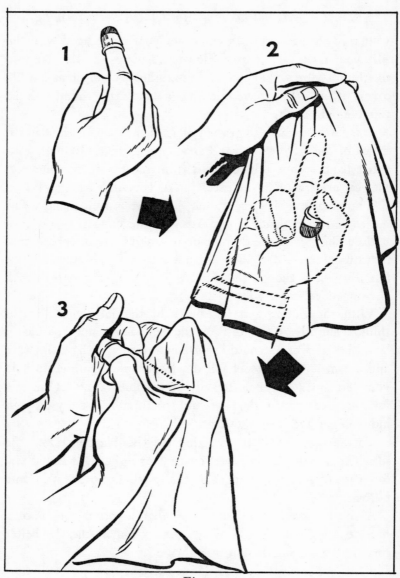

Fig. 9

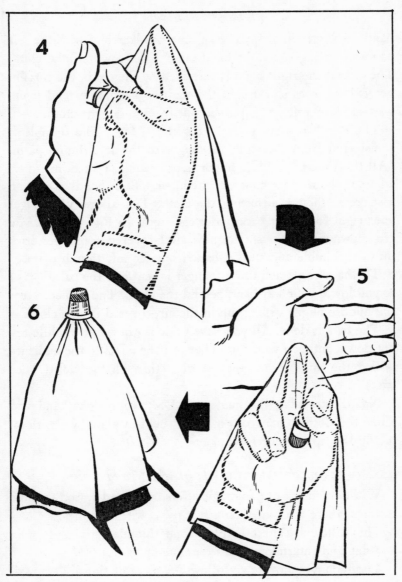

Fig. 10

hand. As shown in #2, you pick up a handkerchief with the left hand and bring the right hand behind the cover of the cloth. The instant the right hand is shrouded by the cloth, the forefinger is bent in as shown and the middle finger is extended upwards. The forefinger is pushed out from under the cloth.

The two hands are brought together (#3). The thimble is transferred from the right forefinger to the left thumb palm. (All this time the middle finger is projecting upward, masquerading as the thimble-covered forefinger.) Both hands are given a shake as though adjusting the cloth. This allows you to get your right forefinger back under the cloth. In Fig. 10, #4, you are shown how to push the now cloth-covered forefinger back into the thimble and steal it back from the left thumb palm.

The hands separate, the forefinger is bent into the palm (#5) as you lower your left hand behind the cloth. The audience sees the middle finger sticking up in the air, covered by the cloth.

The trick is done. All you have to do is draw your middle finger down, and pop your forefinger up; the effect to the audience is that the thimble has popped right through the cloth! (See #6.)

Not illustrated is the final step. Drop your right hand and allow the cloth to hang down freely, held in place by the thimble on the tip of your forefinger.

GHOST THIMBLE [*John A. M. Howie*]

While the literature on magic offers many and varied thimble routines, there are remarkably few *tricks* with thimbles.

The following effect employs one thimble only and is an amusing and entertaining item for close-up work.

The requirements are as follows: A piece of tinfoil (approximately three inches by two inches in size) in the left coat pocket, a long pencil or miniature wand in the breast pocket, and a thimble in the right coat pocket. The thimble should be of aluminum or silver and have a layer of tinfoil neatly glued over its outer surface.

The plot deals with an invisible thimble, the existence of which the performer apparently proves beyond all doubt. The sequence of moves is divided into four phases for ease of description. In practice, these phases blend smoothly to give a complete effect.

Phase I—Pantomime: While proclaiming that you possess an invisible thimble, reach into the right coat pocket and thumb palm the thimble. Bring out the right hand with the forefinger extended as though bearing a thimble on its tip. Act throughout as though the thimble really exists. "Remove" it from the right forefinger between the left forefinger and thumb and "display" it to the spectators. Then "replace" it. If desired, you can pantomime a simple vanish of thimble from the left hand followed by reproduction from the left elbow "to show how simple thimble magic is, provided the thimble is invisible."

Phase II—Taps: Close the left hand into a fist, palm downwards, and go through the motions of pushing the invisible thimble into the fist and leaving it there. Take the pencil from the breast pocket with the right hand and push one end into the left fist, simultaneously getting the other end between the right-hand, first and second fingers and into the thumb-palmed thimble. Fig. 11, #1, illustrates this position.

The "invisible" thimble is now audibly tapped with the pencil. What is actually happening is this—the end of the pencil in the left fist is gripped firmly by the tips of the first and second fingers. By sliding the right hand fairly rapidly backward and forward over a short distance, the tapping sound is produced by the pencil tip striking the thumb-palmed thimble. After several taps remove the pencil and replace it in the breast pocket. To

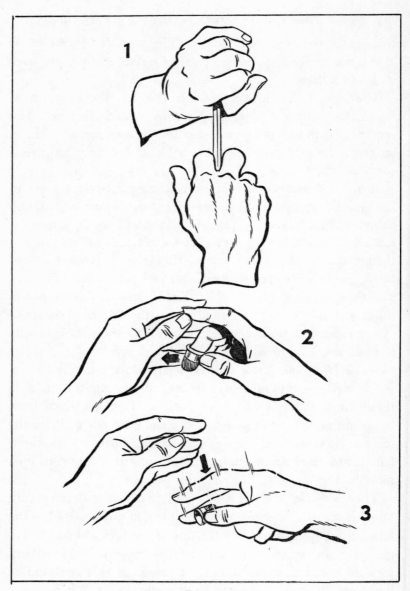

Fig. 11

maintain the illusion, "re-take" the invisible thimble on the tip of the right forefinger.

Phase III—Pop: As further audible proof of the existence of the invisible thimble, it is apparently "popped" as follows: Transfer the thimble from the thumb palm to the tip of the right-hand second finger. Place the tip of the right forefinger between the left forefinger and thumb as shown in #2. The back of the right hand is, of course, to the audience. Hold the left forefinger and thumb rigidly in position and pull the right forefinger downwards as in #3, in imitation of "popping" the thimble supposed to be held between the left forefinger and thumb. Synchronized with this downward pull must be the real "pop," which is made by the second finger tip being levered out of the hidden thimble as it is pressed against the right thumb. The positions just before and just after the secret move are shown in #2 and #3.

If desired, this "pop" effect can be repeated, then the real thimble is again taken on the tip of the right second finger and the "invisible" thimble is "replaced" on the right forefinger tip.

Phase IV—Proof: Having tapped and popped the invisible thimble, you now offer to show its shape. Take the piece of the tinfoil from the left pocket, display it on both sides, then hold it between the hands as in Fig. 12, #4. With the right forefinger extended in front of the tinfoil you can now extend the second finger behind the tinfoil. Hold the thimble against the back of tinfoil with the left thumb and remove the right hand altogether. Now place the right forefinger with its "invisible" thimble behind the tinfoil and into the real thimble. Immediately wrap the tinfoil around the thimble, using the left fingers assisted by the right thumb. This wrapping should be done in such a way that a loose fitting tinfoil shell is formed around the thimble. Surplus tinfoil extending below the rim of the thimble should either be

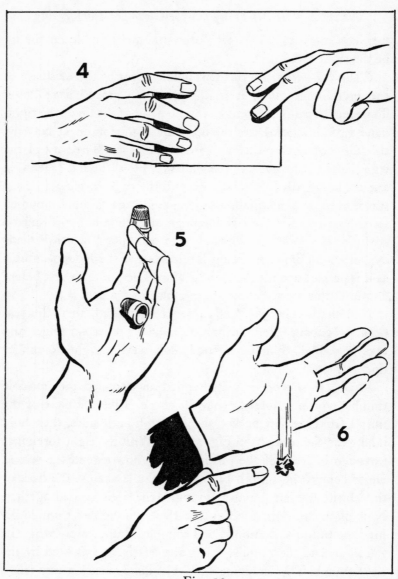

Fig. 12

torn off or folded up and pressed against the rest of the tin foil.

When the shell has been formed, take the thimble plus shell and hold mouth downwards between the left thumb and forefinger. Under cover of the left fingers, allow the thimble to fall down to the base of the fingers as in #5. Take the shell on the tip of the right forefinger. Display it, then apparently transfer it to the left hand. Actually during this movement, thumb-palm the shell in the right hand and open the left hand to display the solid thimble. This thimble can then be bounced on the hand, tapped on the table, etc., to prove that the invsisble thimble is really solid.

During these moves the right hand hangs naturally at your side. Let the tinfoil shell fall to the finger palm, roll it into a ball and nip it between the second and third finger tips. With the thimble resting on the upturned left hand, reach over and remove it with right hand, leaving the ball of tinfoil in its place and hidden by the slightly bent fingers. Move the thimble onto the right, forefinger tip.

Hold the right hand, back to the audience, with the extended forefinger pointing to the left. Cover the forefinger with the left hand and immediately thumb-palm the thimble and re-extend the forefinger. Remove the left hand as though scraping the tinfoil off the invisible thimble. Make a crumpling motion with the left hand, then open hand to show the tinfoil as in #6.

Your patter during this last move should be along these lines: "Of course, if I scrape off the tinfoil (cover forefinger) then the thimble is again invisible (show bare forefinger) without its cloak of tinfoil." (Open left hand and drop tinfoil to table.)

"Remove" the invisible thimble, then "return" it to the right hand which puts it away in the pocket (leave real thimble behind).

BOLT AND FRAME [*G. Legman*]

This false penetration of the bolt through the frame makes an interesting paper-folding illusion, and with the loose ends at the back folded over each other, it can be handed around as a puzzle (Fig. 13). A finger tip or pencil can be poked (half-way) under the bar and frame at every side to show that the bar passes freely through the frame. A surprise ending is also given, which transforms the completed folding into Cleopatra's Barge (Fig 14).

Use plain or striped paper; begin with decorated side up (Fig. 13).

Fold corner A to center of diagonal line (#1).

Now pull point A further along toward B, until folded line DE falls along the center diagonal line (#2).

Fold point A back again on the center line. Now, instead of repeating steps #1 and #2 with point B, fold B over to fall point A. This is to save time (#3).

Fold point B back (top layer only) on center line (#4).

Fold work *backward* along AB, as indicated by dot-dash line (#5).

Lay work down as shown in #6. Fold A and B up to center point D. *Unfold.*

This key step is the "box-making" fold. Bring point D (left side) out and down to A, and point D′ (right side) out and down to B, as the arrows show, spreading apart D and D′ with your forefingers or thumbs. Point C will fall toward you like a skirt, creating a flat waist-line at FG (#7).

Repeat steps #6 and #7 on the other side of the work, being careful to use the top layer only (#8).

Fold in points D and D′, and point C, to meet. Repeat on other side (#9).

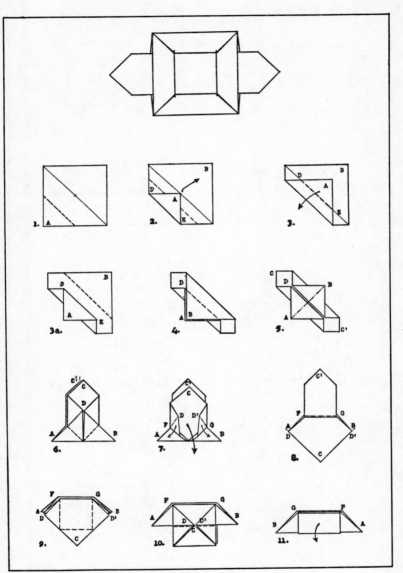

Fig. 13

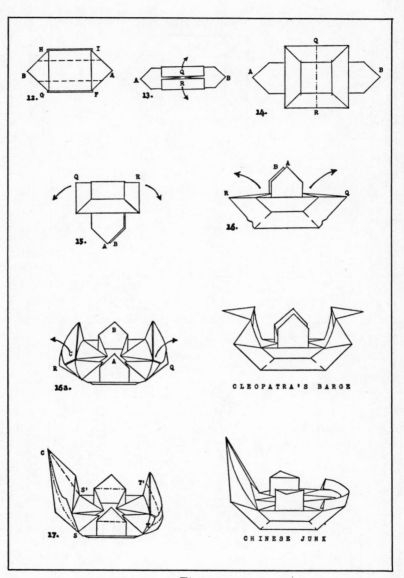

Fig. 14

Fold up the bottom flap (top layer only) on line AB. Repeat on other side (#10).

Open work downward on line BA, folding two layers forward and two layers back (#11).

Fold GF up to center line BA (top layer first, and neatly— this is the bolt—then the layer underneath). Fold HI down to center line, also one layer at a time. *Turn work over* (Fig. 14, #12).

Open frame by spreading top and bottom layers and inner points apart, creasing neatly at the corners (#13).

Cleopatra's Barge is now made in three quick steps (Fig. 14). A similar form, called the Chinese Junk, is well known, having first been shown in the West in T. de Moulidar's *Grande Encyclopédie . . . des Jeux* (1888), p. 339. An even better form is shown in Kodo Kawarasaki's "Origami Moyo," (*Paper-Folding Designs,* Kyoto, 1935) vol. 1: p. 28, but without directions. The form shown here is new.

Fold the Bolt and Frame *backward* on line QR (Fig. 14, #14).

Hold the work, at Q and R (a little in from the points), and pull gently out and down, first Q then R, as the arrows show (#15).

Turn work upside down. Draw up the top layer at each end, from the crack in the seat, and turn out the points to make the prow and stern (#16).

To change the Barge into a Junk, fold the prow inward on lines CS and CS', to make the sail. Fold in the stern on line TT' for the taffrail. Bend side points out (#17).

To restore the Bolt and Frame: Spread open the front and back seats of Cleopatra's Barge at the knees, letting the prow and stern fall inward. Turn over, and you have #14 again.

Pull simultaneously at both ends, and the figure disappears.

THE LOTUS [*G. Legman*]

The paper folding known to magicians as the Bow-tie (Fig. 16) is actually the Lover's Knot or Lotus. It is described in Mrs. W. Campbell's *Paper Toy Making* (London: Isaac Pitman, 1937) p. 40, the best manual of paper-folding in English. This gives the standard fold.

Here is a new and better method, giving the Lotus four petals instead of two, and hiding the loose ends so the spectator can be challenged to take the Lotus apart without tearing it. A surprise solution is also given.

Use an eight inch square of paper or larger. If it is decorated on one side only, begin steps #1 and #3 with the undecorated side facing up. Observe all turnings-over of the work as indicated. They are important.

Fold diagonal AB. Open. Fold other diagonal CD. Open. *Turn work over* (Fig. 15, #1).

Fold across EF. Open. Fold across GH. Open. *Turn over* (#2).

That side of the paper should be facing up on which the diagonals show as valleys and the cross-lines as mountains (#3).

Fold all corners to the center. Unfold these (#4).

(For speed combine this with #4.) Fold corners H to line JK in #4. Then fold over to center on line JK. Do this with all four corners. You now have #5. *Turn over*. Other side is #6.

Fold all corners to center, as in #7.

Turn over. You now have #8.

This is the key fold. Squeeze work in half toward you, allowing the side corners to pop up. Thus: Squeeze together points L and M with left thumb and forefinger, allowing line LM to pop up. Simultaneously, squeeze together points N and O with

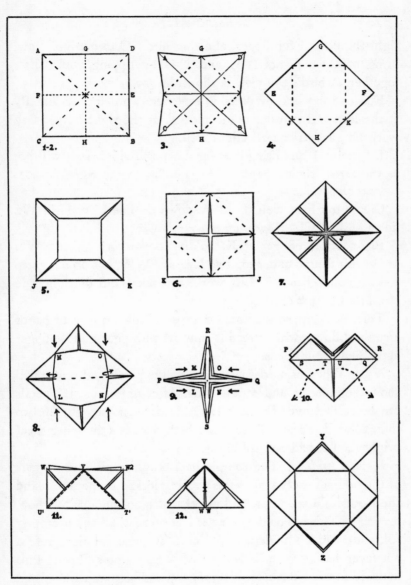

Fig. 15

right thumb and forefinger, allowing line NO to pop up. Now, bring together points L-M and N-O by tipping your wrists together. A bird's eye view is shown in #9.

Flatten the work, by pressing together two points (S and P) at the left, and two points (R and Q) at the right (#9). Lay work flat, and crease all edges well.

Lift point T and bring it as far down to the left as it will go, as the arrow shows. Same with point U, to the right (#10). *Repeat on other side.*

Crease top lines well. Fold W down on line U'V. Fold W2 down on line VT'. *Repeat on other side* (#11).

Place left forefinger at X, holding down both W and W2. Insert left thumb under top two layers at WW, but do *not* grasp hidden points beneath. Lift work, and take hold of right side too. Hold on (#12).

Turn WW up, so spectators can see it. Now bring your hands apart and down, while pressing upward with your middle finger at V. The Lotus opens.

Note: When using decorated paper, the petals and center will show the inner or undecorated side. After unfolding, the petals can be folded over the center. Or fold the Lotus out of two thin, colored sheets held together back to back (the inner sheet bright red) for a beautiful unfolding.

Puzzle Ending: The completed Lotus has all four corners of the original sheet (the petals) visibly locked at the top. Hand the Lotus to a spectator, and ask that it be taken apart without tearing it. This *can* be done, but is laborious, as all the operating folds are hidden underneath. For a surprise solution, refold whatever has been unfolded, or do a new Lotus. Then: Pull outward firmly but smoothly on the top and bottom points Y and Z (either with or without the petals). This will also open the Lover's Knot.

LOTUS AND BOW-TIE [*G. Legman*]

Two bow-ties folded from dollar bills, with Washington's face in the knot, are described in the magic literature. The first is by Mitchell Dyszel, on a renewal circular for Ted Annemann's *Jinx* in 1942 entitled "Bow Knot Money." It is an ingenious variant of the Lover's Knot, but is extremely complex and ends up very small. The other, in the mimeographed "Bill Folds" published by Snyder's Magic Company in Cleveland in 1945, was developed by Al O'Hagan. This also ends up small, with a narrow knot, and the back side of the bill forward.

Here is a new bow-tie, folded from a dollar bill (Fig. 16). It is simpler to make than either of the others, and also looks more like a real bow-tie (although the audience sometimes identifies it as spectacles). As people often try to pull the bow-tie apart, an extra step is given to prevent this.

Lay bill with green back up. Fold edge CD to AB, folding along center-line EF. *Unfold* (Fig. 16, #1-2).

Fold all corners to center-line EF (#3).

Fold edges IJ and GH to EF. All the green of the bill is now hidden (#4).

Fold in half downward, along EF (#5).

Fold point E over on F. Flatten out the top layer from underneath, while bringing point E down at right angles to KF as shown on by the dotted lines (#6).

Repeat step #6 on other side, with point F (#7).

Fold up point F beyond K along line LM. Turn work over and repeat with point E (#8).

Fold M′ and L′ to line NE. (The prime marks mean that these are on the opposite side of the work from the original M and L.) Turn work over and repeat, folding M and L to line N′F (#9).

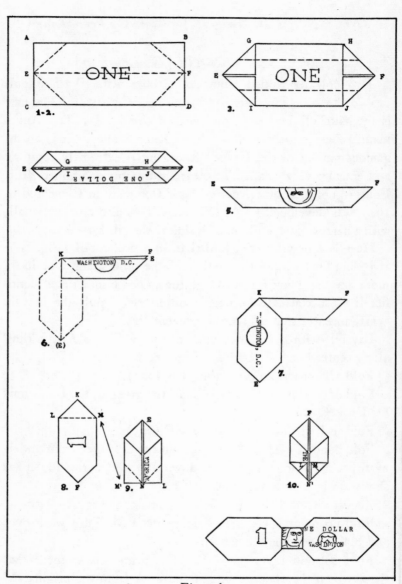

Fig. 16

Hold F with right hand (thumb inside, and forefinger outside, both very low down almost at N). Hold E in the same way with left thumb and forefinger. Open, by bringing your hands apart and down, while pressing up with forefinger tips at N (#10).

Note: Step #10 is described for opening before a spectator, so that Washington's face in the knot will be right side up as viewed. To open for yourself to see, hold F in left hand, E in right.

If the wings of the bow are too extreme to suit your taste, they can be modified in any desired way before the unfolding, for instance by turning points E and F backward, making flat ends.

To restore the bill, simply pull the sides apart. To prevent this from happening: In step #9, fold all four corners slightly beyond the center-line NE or N'F and tuck the overlaps under the next layer down. This makes a barrel-shaped knot which can be lengthened by careful pulling until the bow-tie becomes a propeller.

CHAPTER 2

Conjuring with Coins and Paper Money

Conjuring with coins and bills is of double interest to the average person. He is used to handling these in his everyday life and therefore is astonished to see what can be done with such familiar objects; besides—it is everyone's dream to be able to make money obey commands.

PENNY-TRATION [*Harry Baker*]

A spectator is given seven pennies to hold. The magician causes one penny to penetrate the spectator's hand.

If you do any coin penetration effects, it will help to precede this with a trick in which any coin goes through your hand. Then proceed to confound the spectator by doing it in his hand.

All you need is a sense of timing and the ability to borrow seven pennies. Hold the coins in your cupped left hand. Have a volunteer cup his hand. Pour the pennies into his hand. Have him count the pennies back into your hand, aloud. By this time the fact that there are seven coins involved has been impressed sufficiently so you can proceed with the trick.

Have the spectator hold out his left hand, cup-fashion, and again count the pennies into his hand. Warn him that when you drop the seventh coin, he is to clench his fist quickly.

Performer, using his right hand, takes a coin from his left hand and place it in the spectator's cupped fist. After the first coin, each succeeding coin clinks against those in the spectator's hand. After five pennies have been dropped and the eyes and ears of the spectator are ready for one more—the sixth penny is simply clicked against the others. You don't have to palm it out. Just click it and bring it right out again, holding it between the thumb and forefinger. The last penny you throw from your left hand. The spectator closes his fist, you immediately grasp the back of his hand with your right hand. The spectator's hand with six coins is held with its back to the floor; your right hand with one coin in the palm grasps his fist from below.

Cup your hand a trifle so that the penny is not in contact with his hand. Dilate on your prowess and the difficulty of causing a coin to penetrate solid flesh. Slowly bring your coin up into contact with the back of his hand and cue him into admitting that he has felt the coin penetrate his hand. Show your penny and have him count his six—and immediately go into your next trick.

Note: The back of the hand does not have many sensory nerves. Therefore, when you want the spectator to feel the coin bring it into contact with his knuckles, which are rich in tactile development.

WRAPAROUND VANISH

With a half dollar in your left hand trouser pocket, borrow a half dollar from a spectator. Hold the borrowed coin pressed against a fold of cloth in your trousers as shown in Fig. 17, #1. Use both the left and right hand fingers to make the cloth fold. Hold the coin against the cloth and the right thumb.

Bring the cloth up and around the coin, hiding it, and forming a trough that is higher on the right than the left hand side. Allow gravity to roll the coin from your right hand to your left, under cover of the cloth, #2.

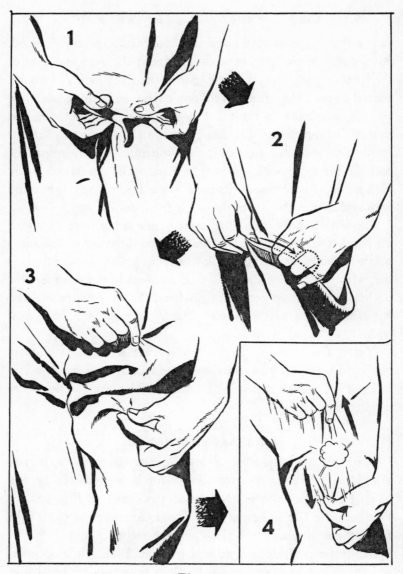

Fig. 17

Release your hold on the cloth and grasp it above and below the fold you have made as in #3. Pull the hands apart, making the cloth open wide.

The effect is as in #4; the coin has vanished—almost visibly. With the coin palmed in the left hand use both hands to press down on the cloth of your trousers and show the form of the half dollar which was previously placed in the pocket.

Claim that the coin really did not vanish. Instead, it penetrated the cloth. Reach into the pocket, bring out the palmed coin and return it to the spectator.

The reason for showing the pocketed coin through the cloth is to take suspicion away from the hands. If you just vanished the coin the spectators would have a right to want to see your hands. Before they can think of this, you throw them off the track by your pretense that the coin has penetrated the cloth of your trousers.

FADEAWAY

One of the first coin tricks I ever learned involved the complete vanish of a half dollar from the top of my thigh.

In performing, place a half dollar on the right thigh as shown in Fig. 18, #1. Prior to performance, under guise of adjusting your trousers, form a fold in the cloth as shown in #1. The fold should make a trough that extends from just behind the knee all the way down to the crotch. This is your only "gimmick."

Bring the right hand, fingers extended but relaxed, down over the coin as in #1 and #2. Under cover of the pretense that you are gently massaging the coin with the palm of your hand, move the coin off the top of the thigh and allow it to slide down into the cloth trough as shown by the dotted line in #2. When you know that the coin has slid down the trough and

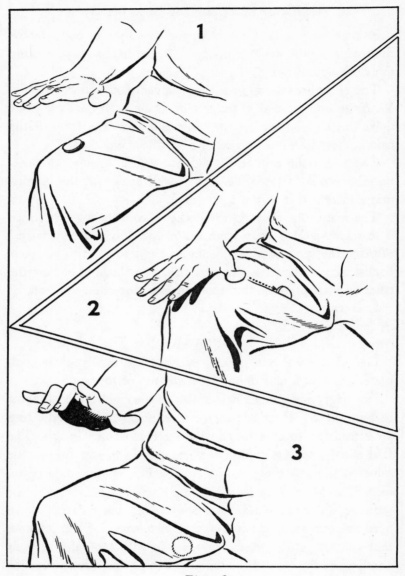

Fig. 18

is securely hidden in the cloth as shown in #3, continue the massaging action with your hand and slowly bring the hand away, showing that the coin has vanished.

This method was always effective and I liked to use it to conclude a series of cloth acquitments and vanishes. It made a good conclusion because the hands were empty, and the coin could be recovered later after a suitable pause.

The late, great Nate Leipzig employed a completely different presentation for this very coin vanish when performing for magicians.

The mechanics were identical, the effect different.

In Leipzig's handling, the trick was preceded by a discussion of the difficulty of palming a coin without revealing the presence of the palmed coin to an observant spectator because of the awkward position demanded by the palming of the coin.

Leipzig would then place the coin on his knee and pick it up in the classic palm, showing how the back of his hand had to curve in order to hold the coin in place.

He would then place his hand back on his thigh, allowing the coin to slide down into the cloth trough as he went on to say, "That was the way my hand used to look when I palmed a coin. But no longer. I have developed a new palm."

With the coin already vanished he would lift his hand, the fingers relaxed and no tell-tale curve to the back of his hand as shown in #1 and #3. With his hand raised ten or twelve inches from his knee he would say, "You see? There is no rigidity, no way a spectator can tell a coin is palmed."

At that point, with his magician-audience fascinated by what they thought was a completely new palm, he would suddenly and surprisingly slap his hand down onto his thigh and turn the palm of his hand uppermost as he said, "And the best part of this palm is that you can vanish the coin any time you want to!"

SITTING VANISH [*Bill Simon*]

Here is a coin trick that can be done even if you can't palm a thing. In addition, it's a lot more convincing than many more difficult moves. It can only be done while seated but it can be done with any coin.

Fig. 19, #1, shows the way you place the coin on the top of your right thigh with your left hand. Next both hands come towards the coin. Your right hand rotates up on its side as shown, and simultaneously your left hand comes over and pretends to pick up the coin. What really happens is that as the left hand makes its pretense, the right hand, still up on its side, moves forward a trifle and masks the fact that the coin is left in place (#2).

There is no coin in your right hand nor can one be seen on your thigh, which is convincing "proof" that it must be in your left hand.

"Vanish" the coin from your left hand. Next, your right hand (which has remained on your right thigh masking the coin) pushes the coin away from your body to the outside of your thigh as in #3. Your left hand reaches down along the cloth of your trouser leg as in #3 and catches the coin as it is knocked off your thigh by the back of your right hand. Catching the coin, make a pretense of pulling it through the cloth as in #3. The spectators, of course, are on the other side of you, where they cannot see this.

Here is an alternate, perhaps preferable, ending. Place a similar coin in your right trouser cuff before you start. Go through the pretense of a vanish as before and finish by showing the coin in your cuff. Pick it out of your cuff with your left hand, which provides ample cover for you to pick the coin off your thigh with your right hand.

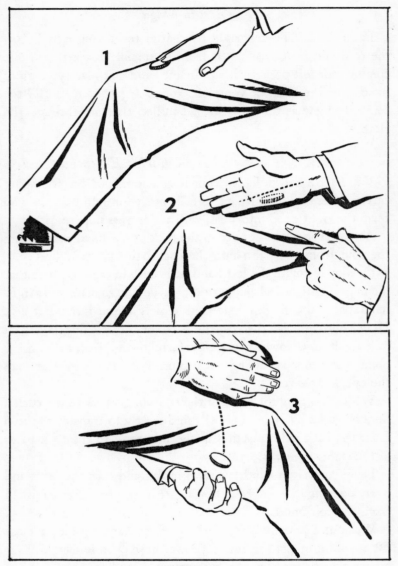

Fig. 19

Palm the coin in your right hand after recovering it and show the coin you have just taken from your cuff. Place the visible coin in your left pocket with your left hand and place your right hand over the cloth of your left trouser leg pocket. "Pull" the coin into view as though you had pulled the coin through the cloth.

BACK PALM SWITCH [*Charles Eastman*]

You have a half dollar in your left hand. Hold it at the finger tips and display it, then let it fall into your left palm as you form the right hand into a fist, with the fingers uppermost.

As you turn your fist over so the back of the hand is up, bring the coin from the palm into the back palm position (Fig. 20, #1). Slowly rotate the left hand, still held in a loose fist so that the fingers will again be uppermost. As you do so, turn your right hand palm up, fingers extended loosely toward the left fist. Drag your right hand across the backs of the left fingers as you talk about how slowly you are performing the trick, making the point that magic is baffling not because the hand is quicker than the eye, but slower.

While dragging the backs of the right fingers across the curled fingers of the left hand you will find it easy to transfer the coin from the back palm position in the left hand to the back palm of the right. (See #1.)

Drop your right hand as shown in #2 and turn the left hand over, opening the fingers, showing that the coin has vanished from the left hand.

Without a pause, slowly curl the right hand up into a loose fist as shown in #3 and bring it toward the open left hand. This allows you to transfer the back-palmed coin from the back of the right hand to the thumb crotch. As the right hand approaches the left, drop the coin out of it into the left hand which

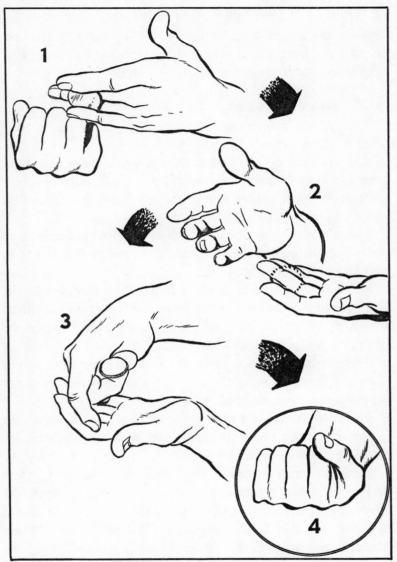

Fig. 20

closes to receive it (#4). Gesture at the left fist with the now empty right hand and slowly open the left hand showing that the vanished coin has returned.

SILVER-COPPER [*Dr. Theodore Sack*]

The greatest close-tricks are those wherein the magic takes place in the spectator's hands.

You will need two English pennies (these are copper and the same size as an American half dollar) and a half dollar.

Begin with one copper coin in the left hand, the half dollar and a copper coin in the right hand.

The whole purpose of the trick is to keep the audience from suspecting the existence of the second copper coin. Here is an easy way to deny this suspicion.

Hold the copper coin in the left hand, at the base of the fingers (see Fig. 21, #1, where only one copper coin is shown for clarity). Open the right hand showing the half dollar on top of the copper coin in that hand.

Bring the right hand to the left and retain the copper coin in the right hand, allowing the silver coin to drop on top of the copper coin in the left hand.

The effect is that you have shown a copper and a silver coin in the right hand and transferred them to the left. Two coins and only two coins have been seen.

Retain the unseen copper coin at the base of the right fingers as you point out the curious relationship between copper and silver. Say these two metals were widely used in medieval alchemy, and that certain magical powers still, even in these atomic days, remain in these metals.

Make sure that the silver coin in the left hand is at the base of the fingers, and retain it there as you toss the copper coin into the right hand to join the copper coin already there.

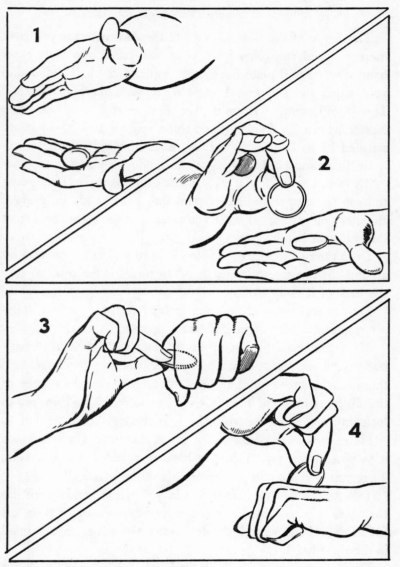

Fig. 21

The jingle of the coins is proof to the audience that you have merely tossed the coins from your left hand into your right hand. Say, "I will place the copper coin and the half dollar into your hand, sir. But first I must make sure of your reflexes." This is important, so stress it. Ask the spectator to see how fast he can make a fist. Have him do this a few times. When you are satisfied he will follow directions, have him hold his palm out toward you and hold your right hand over his palm.

"Now remember," you say, "at the count of three, I am going to drop the copper and silver coins into your hand. To prevent chicanery on my part, I want you to enclose the coins the instant they hit your hand."

Drop the two copper coins into his hand and as he makes a fist around them, use your right hand to turn his fist over so that the back of it is uppermost.

He can feel two distinct coins in his hand, but no tactile impression can tell him that both are copper.

Have him hold his fist up about even with his coat's breast pocket and ask him to reach into his fist with the forefinger and thumb of his other hand and remove either coin, the copper or the silver, at random. That is, he is just to remove a coin, not to look into his fist to see which he is removing.

He removes one of the two coins as shown in #3 and hands it to you as you say, "Ah, you have removed the copper coin. That means you retain the silver half dollar! Good."

Take the copper coin from him in your right hand which has the silver coin palmed. Place the copper coin on top of your left fist as shown in #4, which also shows the silver coin palmed in the right hand.

Have the spectator clench his fist firmly around what he thinks is the silver coin as you turn the copper coin over and over on the back of your left fist with your right fingers.

Emphasize that he has the silver coin—you have the copper coin. Pick up the copper coin at your finger tips and gesture at his fist with the coin.

"Watch!" you say loudly. "Open your hand! The silver coin has left your hand . . ." As he opens his hand and sees that he holds a copper coin, not a silver one as he thought, you will be able to switch the copper coin for the palmed silver one by turning your left hand over palm up and dropping the palmed half dollar into your left palm as the right finger tips pull the visible copper coin up into the right palm (#2).

Have him hold up his coin for all to see as you use your right finger tips to pick up the visible coin from your left palm and display it. The fact that you are holding the coin at your finger tips will disguise the fact that you are holding the palmed coin, since holding the visible coin gives reason for your right hand to be curved. In effect, the visible coin serves the same function that the magic wand did in the old days when magicians were able to use it to cover the fact that something was secreted in the hand that held the wand.

HANK DROPPER [*E. Brian MacCarthy*]

Buried away in a manuscript by E. Brian MacCarthy, one of England's most inventive sleightsters, was a very pleasant conceit involving an unprepared handkerchief and some coins.

In the course of experimenting with MacCarthy's idea I developed a handling that makes his method a little easier of execution. Since the effect is one capable of endless development I can only give a brief idea of the possibilities inherent in it. Bear in mind, however, that this is a utility device with many uses.

Place a gentleman's handkerchief on the table in front of you as in Fig. 22, #1. Bring end C up to A as shown in #2. Next

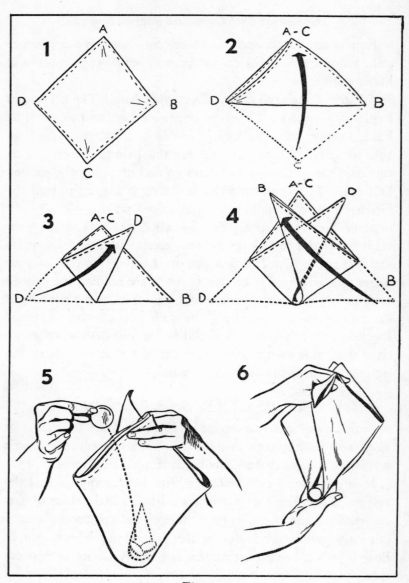

Fig. 22

bring end D over A-C as in #3. Finally, bring end B over D and A-C, as shown in #4.

Pick up the handkerchief in the left hand with ends A-C between the middle and ring fingers as shown in #5. The ends labeled B-D are held between the thumb and forefinger.

Clearly shown in #4 is a fold of cloth formed at the lower point of the folded handkerchief. This is the "gimmick" upon which the effect depends. Be sure to hold the ends B-D higher than the ends A-C. (I found that this makes the effect work more precisely than in MacCarthy's handling.)

With the handkerchief held as described, drop four coins, half dollar size, into the handkerchief, between A-C and D-B. Instead of being securely held inside the handkerchief as it appears, the coins will drop into the little fold at the base of the handkerchief as shown in #5 and #6.

Jiggle the handkerchief and the coins will jingle, offering "proof" that they are in the handkerchief.

Bring the handkerchief over the other hand, and jingle the coins again, by letting them clash against the palm of the outstretched hand as in #6.

Up to this point you have been holding the inner two points of the handkerchief (B-D) higher than the outer ones. Reverse this, lifting A-C higher than the inner ones, and the fold of cloth where the coins are held will open wide as shown in #6, allowing the coins to slide from the handkerchief into your waiting right hand.

To the audience, all you have done is clink the coins through the cloth against your right palm. Really, the coins are now gone from the handkerchief.

Allow the right hand to lift up and take a single corner of the handkerchief in the left hand; then rip it away from the left hand and toss the handkerchief into the air.

The effect, as the cloth flutters down, is a pretty one, for seemingly the coins vanish in mid-air.

As the cloth falls to the floor, reach into the air with your right hand and allow the coins to clink, one against the other.

As soon as the noise of the coins is heard by the audience, let them drop one at a time from your hand to the floor, or to a tray where they will reverberate as they make their presence known.

The effect is that of four coins vanishing from the handkerchief and appearing in your right hand.

An additional and more subtle use of MacCarthy's basic idea is to take advantage of the fact that, if you drop two coins into the section where you can "steal" them and two coins between corners A-C of the handkerchief, you can steal two coins and leave two in the 'kerchief.

A little experimentation will prove that here is a most innocent, most valuable utility device.

REWARD [*John A. M. Howie*]

This item is designed for use with a borrowed handkerchief and is best suited to drawing room or small audience conditions. In effect, a pocket handkerchief is borrowed and used for some other trick and then two half dollars are magically produced from it. These two coins are wrapped in the cloth and held in place by a rubber band. The handkerchief is tossed to the owner who finds, on unwrapping it, two English pennies in place of the silver coins.

Stack two pennies on top of two half dollars and slip a small rubber band around the lot to keep them in position. This stack is in the left pocket. While asking for a handkerchief, place the left hand in the pocket, grip the stack in the finger palm (so the halves are uppermost) and push off the band.

Perform some trick with the handkerchief—the wand through cloth is ideal for this, the coins being well out of sight and not interfering in any way with the effect.

Having shown the handkerchief to be undamaged, leave it draped over the left hand and slide one half dollar up with the thumb. "Notice" the shape and grip the coin through the cloth with the right hand. Turn the right hand over to reverse the handkerchief and reveal the coin. Push the left hand up under the cloth and lay the coin aside. Repeat the production for the second half dollar.

Now lay the handkerchief over the left hand and place both halves upon it. Fig. 23, #1, illustrates the position diagrammatically. The most effective way of reaching this position is to place the first coin on the handkerchief (taking care not to clink against the pennies) then to spin the second coin in the air and catch it on top of the other on the handkerchief.

Bend the left fingers inward to bring the pennies approximately above the halves and grip the four coins through the cloth as in #2, then lift coins and handkerchief completely off the left hand. With a slight shake replace the cloth on the left hand—the relative position of the coins will now be as in #3.

Tap your right pocket with your right hand, then "remember" that you have a rubber band in your left pocket. Gather the hanging corners of the handkerchief in your right hand and raise this hand above the other, carrying away the pennies and leaving the halves in the left finger palm. Take the hand away from the left pocket, leaving the halves behind, and slip the band around the cloth as shown in #4.

Finally toss the handkerchief to the spectator who will be certain to open the package to the amusement of all.

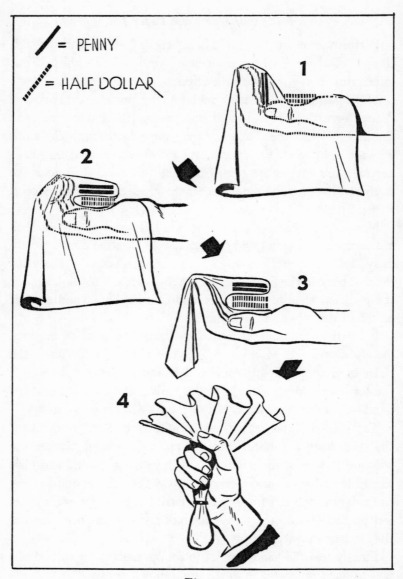

Fig. 23

THE HARD WAY [*Stewart Judah*]

The effect is that you borrow a half dollar, a ring and a handkerchief. Drop the half in the handkerchief and imprison it with the ring around the handkerchief. Two spectators hold the cloth's four ends, as you reach under the handkerchief and release the ring. Impossible! Throw it down in front of them and simultaneously, or nearly so, they see the half dollar in the center of the handkerchief.

The half dollar is placed in the left fingers and thumb and the handkerchief thrown over the coin. Grasp the half through the cloth as in Fig. 24, #1, with the right hand fore and middle fingers, and bring it back a trifle where it is held by the left thumb and forefinger, through the cloth. Drop the hand so the cloth falls down towards the floor while you patter. Give the audience a last look at the coin as in #2 by lifting part of the cloth with the right hand. This shows the coin seemingly under the handkerchief. Really it is on the outside of the handkerchief under a little flap of cloth. This sleight is all the skill you'll need.

Borrow a finger ring and slide it down over the cloth as in #3. This seems to imprison the coin in a cloth pocket. With the ring pulled down firmly you can hold the handkerchief by the ends and show it all around. The cloth is around the coin and hides it perfectly.

Next spread out the cloth as in #4 and have two spectators each hold an end. Show your hand empty and reach under the cloth. You may have to ask for a little slack in order to free the coin. Once it is loose hold the pocket of cloth in the left fingers so that the spectators continue to see the little well in the center of the cloth as in #4.

Grasp the freed ring between the fore and middle fingers as

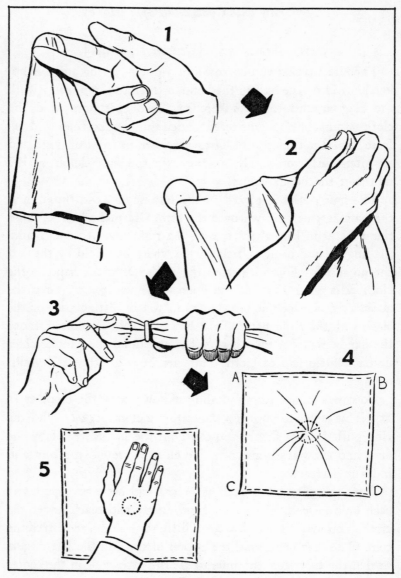

Fig. 24

in #5. Next palm the released coin. Still holding the pocket of cloth from the underneath side in the left fingers, bring the right hand out displaying the ring.

Climax.

All eyes are on the ring. Keep the right hand flat and close to the handkerchief so that as you proffer the ring to the person from whom you borrowed it, you can drop the palmed coin on top of the little well. Release your grasp with the left fingers so the spectators who are holding the ends of the cloth will automatically straighten out the cloth a bit.

To all intents and purposes you have pulled a small diameter ring off the large diameter coin.

NECROMANCY [*Derek Vernon*]

Needed for this excursion into almost pure magic is a topless cigar box or one of similar dimensions as shown in Fig. 25.

For the sake of explanation the trick will be described as though performed with two coins, although the effect can be done with any quantity of small coins.

Your only preparation is to place two coins behind the inverted box, as shown in Fig. 25, #1. Pick up the box by the sides with both hands, as shown. The box shields the coins from almost every angle. As you come down with the box bring it forward as shown in #2. You now have two coins under the box unknown to the spectators.

Borrow two matching coins from the spectators and place them on top of the inverted box as shown in #3.

The only "move" is shown in #4. Having commented on the coins, place the right hand in the position shown and cover the right hand with the left hand. To the audience you seem to be trying to press one of the coins through the solid wood. Under cover of the left hand, the right thumb moves backwards to

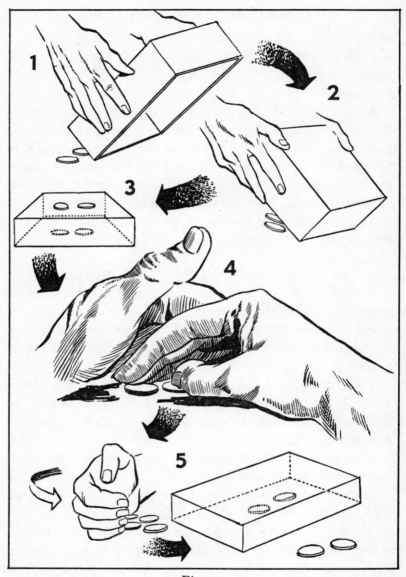

Fig. 25

you, as shown, which pushes the coin off the box. The spectators hear it fall. Repeat with the other coin after lifting hands to show that the first coin has gone.

Lift the box as in #1 by the sides and show that the coins have penetrated the wood. The lifted box masks the borrowed coins that are lying hidden behind the box.

All that remains is to remove the evidence. This is shown in #5. Two things happen simultaneously. Pick up the box with the left hand and, as you do so, sweep the right hand forward to pick up the visible coins. However, the sweep continues and you pick up the hidden coins all in the same movement.

This must be done casually. Once you have the four coins in your hand push the box forward for examination with the other hand. Release the box, bring this hand back, and with it take two coins from the four in the right hand to return to the people from whom you borrowed them.

THE RIP

I have found that, fascinated as most people are by magic, they are equally if not more fascinated by descriptions of the activities of light fingered gentry like the "short-con" men.

One of the most widely used cheating devices of the short-con is short-changing. Most people are not too concerned with the details of the way silver coins are short-counted, but the average audience is interested when you show them how they may have been cheated out of bills.

Take five one-dollar bills out of your pocket in a stack and count them, one—two—three—four—five. Do this slowly and deliberately so that the spectators know that you have five bills.

Stack the bills neatly in your left hand as shown in Fig. 26, #1. Reach toward your left hand with your right hand and, as you do so, push your left thumb up as far as you can toward the

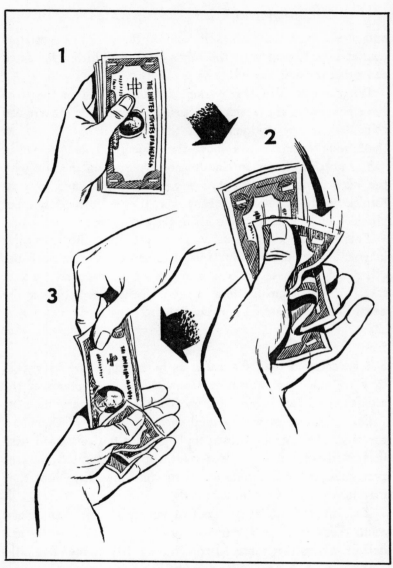

Fig. 26

outer tips of the stack of bills and press down with the ball of your thumb against the top of the top dollar bill. Pull the thumb down as shown by the arrow in #2.

When you pull the bill down, it will crumple on itself as shown. Your right hand comes closer to the extended tips of the bills as shown in #3 and removes the stack of four bills from the left hand as shown.

The right hand offers the bills, just shown to be five in number, to one of the spectators, as the left hand with the crumpled "stolen" bill drops to the side. Have the spectator count the bills. To his surprise, he holds but four.

At this point reveal the bill you have secreted in your left hand.

THE FOLD-AROUND

Having demonstrated how easily the average person can be short-changed by means of "The Rip," take back the four bills from the spectator and add the fifth bill you hold to the stack. Straighten out the crumpled bill you "stole" and hold the bills by their centers in the left hand aat the finger tips and thumb as shown in Fig. 27, #1.

Begin to count the bills again and as you do, say, "One." Fold the outermost bill around the tip of the middle finger as shown in #1. The hands have been shown lifted high for clarity. In performance, they are tilted toward the floor so the spectators cannot see the following process.

As the first bill is folded around the tip of the middle finger at the count of one, the second bill, at the count of two, is brought around from the palm side of the hand toward the back of the fingers. Under cover of this action the tips of the right fingers fold the first bill back on itself (as shown in #2) so that the first bill is now folded in quarters around the tip of the

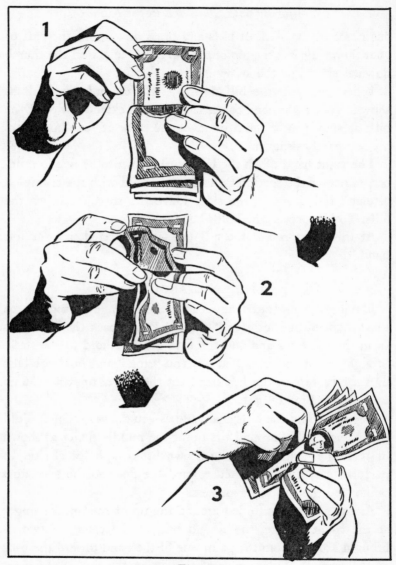

Fig. 27

middle finger. The rest of the bills are counted and brought away from the left hand as in #3. They conceal the folded bill on the tip of the middle finger which is then brought into the palm.

Hand the four bills, which the audience has just seen counted as five, to a spectator to count.

As soon as he realizes that he holds only four bills, reach out with the left hand and pop the folded bill into view, allowing it to unfold as you do so.

Done correctly, the effect is quite magical.

PERFECTION [*H. P. Graham*]

There have been many methods devised to make a dollar bill vanish and reappear inside a lemon. Graham's method comes closest to perfection of any I have ever seen. The primary differences between his method and any other are that there is no switch of the bill and it is the spectator and not the magician who cuts open the lemon and finds his bill inside the fruit. What's more, it is the *spectator* who reads off the serial number from the bill to the person who originally copied down the number.

Fig. 28 shows the basic subtlety upon which the trick depends. Take a dollar bill and cut off a quarter of it as in #1 and #2. Cutting along the lines indicated makes for perfect camouflage. There is one thing to watch. In cutting the bill, preferably with a razor, cut from the back to the front so that the edge of the cut is beveled. The beveling should be at an angle away from the front of the bill. This serves to conceal the line of demarcation.

There is only one other bit of preparation. The bill that you cut must have a serial number which is in series with another bill—that is, you use the old but good gag of changing the last digit of the dollar bill's serial number from a six to an eight by

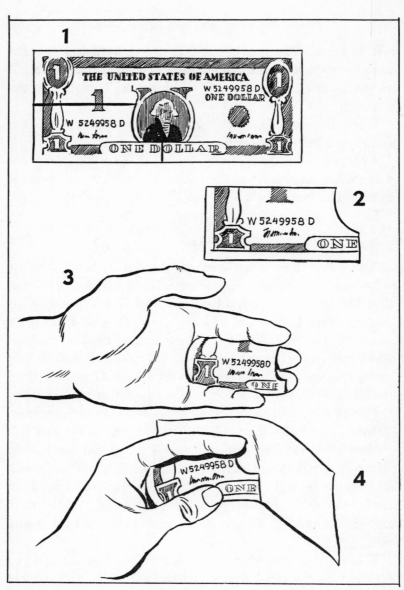

Fig. 28

drawing a loop on the top of the six with India ink to make it look like an eight, or changing a three to an eight similarly.

This gives you two dollar bills with apparently identical serial numbers.

This is very little preparation when you realize that once it is done it never has to be done again. One final note about the bills. When you get them seriatim they are generally brand new. You will have to crumple and dirty the bills till they approximate the wear and tear of an ordinary bill. This applies to the fake, of course.

Fig. 28, #1, shows the way the fake quarter blends in with a borrowed bill. The only sleight you need is shown in #3 and #4. Assume you have borrowed a bill from a helpful spectator. You have three lemons, one loaded with the duplicate bill. You have the fake quarter bill in the position shown in #3, in the left hand.

As you take the borrowed bill from the spectator with the right hand, place it in the left hand under the fake quarter which is hidden there. At this point, when the real bill has not been out of sight for a second, you bring up the business of having the serial number written down. The fake blends in with the real bill, as in #4. There is one point to watch. After you have the real bill and the fake quarter coordinated, flip the right hand end of the real bill back. Don't fold it under as that would be suspicious; just push it back so it is out of eye range.

Indicate the serial number on the fake quarter with the right forefinger as you ask to have the number copied down. Once it is copied, ask the spectator to initial the bill. Again indicate the fake quarter. This time you can bend the projecting end of the bill away as though to give more support for the initialing. The initials, then, go on the fake quarter of a bill.

The fake stays in exactly the same position in the left fingers as the trick proceeds. With your right hand, fold up the borrowed bill, pulling it away from the fake as you fold.

For the vanish, have a dummy bill sewn in a handkerchief. You have someone hold the borrowed, folded bill as you flip your handkerchief open. Once it is open have the spectator put the borrowed bill under the handkerchief. Under cover of this, switch the real bill for the folded dummy sewn in the handkerchief.

Most of your work is done. Vanish the bill by flapping open the handkerchief, having put the borrowed bill in a pocket by this time.

Give spectators a choice of the three lemons. Force the loaded lemon. Hand a knife to a spectator at the other side of the room from the one from whom you borrowed the bill, and have him cut the chosen lemon in half. He discovers the bill in the lemon. Have him open it and read the serial numbers on it. These, of course, coincide with the numbers which were jotted down in the first place. By the way, the loaded bill has a scribble of initialing on it in the same place that you had the spectator do the real initialing.

Now that the serial number has been checked, take the wet bill from this spectator. In taking it, replace your fake quarter bill in top of this bill. You then have the first spectator see that the initials are really his own and there seemingly has been no trickery.

To avoid giving away one of your bills with the fake serial number, apologize for the wetness of the bill that has just been taken from the lemon and give "another" bill back to the spectator. This, of course, is the bill which you originally borrowed.

One final note in the event you have never done the bill in lemon trick. The easiest way to prepare a lemon is to pull the little pip out of the end and, with a pencil, push a hole through the length of the lemon. That done, load in your bill and glue the pip back in place. There is absolutely nothing to reveal that the lemon has been tampered with.

CHAPTER 3

The Magician Performs with Rings, Ropes, and Silks

Although 90 per cent of the tricks in this book can be performed without apparatus of any kind, there are certain tricks which can be done only with special paraphernalia. The only such tricks I have included are those which have so tremendous an effect that this makes up for the need of special gadgets.

Two items that I certainly recommend you buy are the Jardine Ellis Ring Trick and Brema's Nut Trick. These can be purchased at any magic store. The Ellis Ring Trick consists of a solid ring and a shell ring. The Brema Nut Trick is made up of a solid brass nut and a gimmicked nut which can be pulled apart when the trick demands it.

This modest apparatus, which can be bought for less than four dollars, makes possible some astonishing effects which will be described later in this chapter.

BAGUETTE [*Paquette*]

This effect is the simplest, nicest form of the ring-on-the-wand that I have seen. A borrowed finger ring, placed under a handkerchief, vanishes and then appears on a magic wand whose ends are being held by a spectator.

The performer stands with his right side to the spectator, a wand under his left arm as in Fig. 29, #1. Having borrowed

Fig. 29

a finger ring, the performer places it under a handkerchief. The ring is placed under the cloth by the right hand. The left holds the cloth as shown in #2. Just as the right hand, with the ring, passes the left hand under cover of the cloth, the ring is grasped as shown in #2 by the left thumb and pressed against the near edge of the cloth against the fingers of the left hand which are on the other side of the cloth.

The right hand, under the cloth, proceeds forward to the center of the cloth as though still retaining the ring. The right fingers point upward toward the ceiling, higher than the end of the wand which is under the left arm as in #1.

The tip of the wand is higher than the rest of the wand, so that the ring drops back along the wand towards your body. This is screened by the handkerchief.

The left hand takes the handkerchief at the center, as though grasping the ring through the folds of the cloth, while at the same time the right hand comes across the chest and takes the wand from under the left arm pit. At this moment, the right fingers cover the ring on the wand and the wand is brought toward the spectator as you ask him to hold both ends of the wand. By now, of course, the ring on the wand is hidden by the right hand.

As soon as the spectator holds both ends of the wand, bring the handkerchief in the left hand over the center of the wand and take the right hand away. The cloth now hides the fact that the ring is on the wand.

Pause and patter about the difficulty of that which you are about to attempt, then rip the handkerchief away so that it spins the ring around and around as the cloth comes away from the wand.

The effect is as though the ring vanished from under the cloth and instantly reappeared on the center of the wand whose ends are being held tightly!

THUMB FUN [*Franklin V. Taylor*]

Needed for this wonderful trick are the Jardine Ellis' ring, with the fake half shell on it, a handkerchief, and a spectator.

Holding the fake and ring as one, make it clear that your hands are empty but for the "ring" (Fig. 30, #1). Place the ring and shell, as one, on the spectator's thumb as shown in #3. As you put the ring and shell in place on his thumb, with his thumb pointing at the ceiling as shown in #3, press down on the ring as, with the other hand, you remove your pocket handkerchief and throw it over the spectator's thumb and hand.

Don't press too hard, just press firmly.

Next, lift the shell off the ring as you put your hand under the cloth. Leave the cloth over the spectator's thumb, and leave the real ring in place, as shown in #4. The spectator, oddly, will feel you take the shell off his thumb, but if he obeys directions and keeps his hand perfectly still, he will *not* feel the real ring which remains in place on his thumb!

Show the fake shell to the spectator and patter, then vanish the shell by the French drop (#2), and the instant that it has disappeared, touch the real ring on his thumb through the cloth.

Only then, when you touch it, will he feel the ring.

Remove the handkerchief from the spectator's hand with the hand in which you have the fake shell concealed, stuff the handkerchief back in your breast pocket, getting rid of the fake as you do so, and with the other hand take the real ring off the spectator's thumb.

The effect is that you vanish the ring and make it reappear on the spectator's thumb under the cloth.

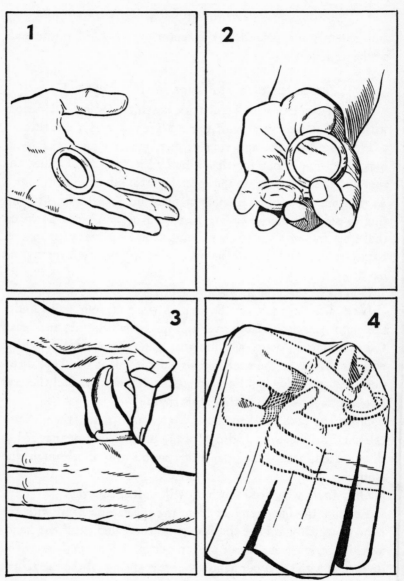

Fig. 30

BREMA PLUS TAYLOR

You'll need the gimmicked Brema Nut, the ungimmicked one, a length of string, a handkerchief, and a finger ring.

Show the real nut and have it examined. The fake nut is finger palmed in your right hand. Have a spectator on your right examine the nut, while a spectator on your left looks at the ring. Then take the nut from the spectator on the right and give him the string, and give the nut to the spectator on the left. In taking these back from the spectators it is simple to switch in the fake nut.

Have the spectators hold the ends of the string and throw a handkerchief over the center of the string. Palm the real nut when taking out the handkerchief. Put your hand under the handkerchief—remove the fake nut and replace the real nut on the string by encircling it in two loops.

Claim that you have done the impossible. Remove the handkerchief, saying that you have removed the nut from the string. You have failed, because the nut seems to be on the string. But, with the two ends of the string still held by two spectators, have a third spectator unloop the nut.

The nut comes off the string in the third spectator's hand. The fake nut goes into your pocket.

While this surprise takes place, put both your hands behind your back, remove your finger ring, and place it on the tip of your thumb as shown in Fig. 31, #1. With the ring in this position and the thumb bent in to the palm, it will be unseen.

Take one end of the string from the spectator with your right hand, and with the left hand slip the ring off your thumb, as shown in #2. It will be found in perfect position to be loaded on the string. (Try this excellent move for the ring-on-the-wand.)

73

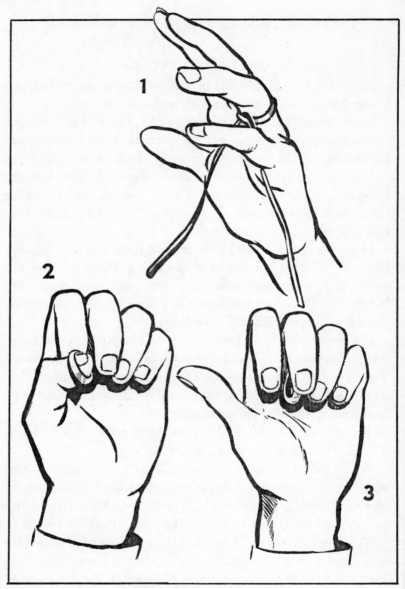

Fig. 31

Pass the string through the left hand (really through the palmed ring) and have the spectator hold the end of the string again, as you claim that you are going to do the really impossible! You are going to place the nut back on the string despite the fact that the ends of the string are held by the spectators.

Observe the conditions. The spectators see a string held by two spectators. Your left hand is holding a part of the string, but that seems incidental. The brass nut is on the table or held by a spectator. This is the real brass nut so no prying eye can detect anything.

Now throw the handkerchief over your left hand and pick up the nut with your right hand. With your right hand replace the finger ring on your ring finger and then loop the brass nut on the string.

Whip off the handkerchief and claim you have replaced the brass nut on the string. Of course the spectator finds that the nut is not on the string at all. As it comes out of the loops lift your left hand in surprise and say that you can't understand why the nut is not on the string.

Let the spectators discover that your finger ring is now incomprehensibly on the string (#2).

You are completely clean. The faked nut was only in evidence briefly, and at the finale all that the spectators can find to examine is a real brass nut, an ungimmicked finger ring, and an ordinary length of string.

ELLIOTT ON ELLIS

The effect of this particular presentation of the Jardine Ellis ring trick is simply stated. A silk handkerchief is looped around one's felt middle finger and a metal harness ring is dropped down over the ends of the silk as in Fig. 32, #1.

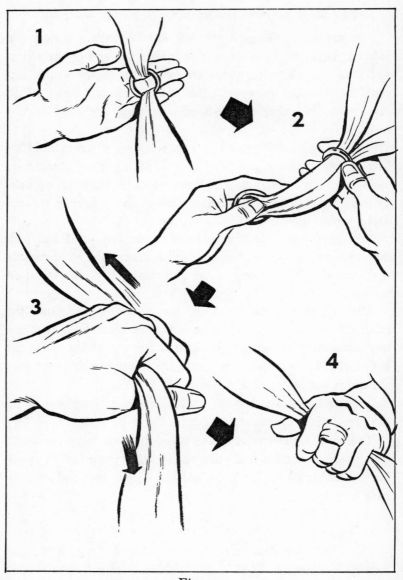

Fig. 32

The ring is removed from the silk by the other hand as shown in #2. The ends of the silk are held by two spectators while the magician places the visible ring under cover of the left hand. An incantation or two, and then, despite the fact that the spectators still retain their hold on the silk's ends, the ring is now on the silk again, as in #1.

The finger is removed and, of course, the ring falls and all may be examined.

Needed are a silk handkerchief, the Ellis ring, and its gimmick—the shell ring. For the first step, the ring and its shell are placed as one on the silk as shown in #1.

Retaining the real ring on the silk by the pressure of the slightly closed fingers of the left hand, the right-hand fingers and thumb pick up the shell ring as in #2 and drag it off the silk.

This handling can and must be done very casually. The existence of the real ring on the silk is concealed by the merest tilting of the fingers of the left hand. All attention is directed to the shell ring as it is being removed from the silk.

As soon as it is free of the silk, the performer has the spectators hold the ends of the silk while the left hand is held back uppermost as in #4.

The right hand brings up the shell ring and, under cover of the left fingers pretends to fuss there, as though doing something. The right hand comes away with the shell ring finger-palmed, and before the spectators have time to want to see the right hand, the left hand is run up and down the silk as in #3 a few times and then finally is turned uppermost as in #1, showing that somehow the ring has been trapped on the silk.

This supplies enough cover to allow you either to "sleeve" the shell ring, or preferably, simply to drop it into the right jacket pocket.

FADEAWAY [*Dai Vernon*]

In this beautiful effect, a firmly tied double knot seems veritably to melt away, leaving not the slightest trace of its former existence.

Trick can be done with two handkerchiefs of any material—borrowed pocket handkerchiefs for impromptu work, or silks for club and stage. Begin by crossing one end over the other as in Fig. 33, #1, gripping the crossing point firmly with left thumb and tip of middle finger. Note that end A is considerably shorter than end B.

Twist B forward around A, apparently forming a knot as in #2. Actually, this is a pseudo-knot, held in place by the left thumb and middle finger. Note that the right hand grips the cloth below the knot by the third and fourth fingers only, leaving the first two fingers free for manipulating the ends.

The left forefinger pushes end A to the right, while the right fingers push B to the left, in back of A, as in #3. Grip the crossing point between thumb and middle finger. Next the right forefinger twists end B back around A and the tip of the finger pushes B through the opening, to form the second knot. Pull the knot tight, gripping the handkerchiefs as shown in #4. The hands may be jerked apart vigorously several times to convince everyone that the double knot is being pulled as tight as possible.

The left hand now grasps the left side of the knot between thumb and forefinger, while the right hand reaches below to grasp handkerchief B. This is shown in Fig. 34, #5. Raise the handkerchief to the right, as shown in #6, jerking it a few times as though tightening the knot further.

If your left hand is holding only the left side of the knot, you will find that the act of raising handkerchief B will bring

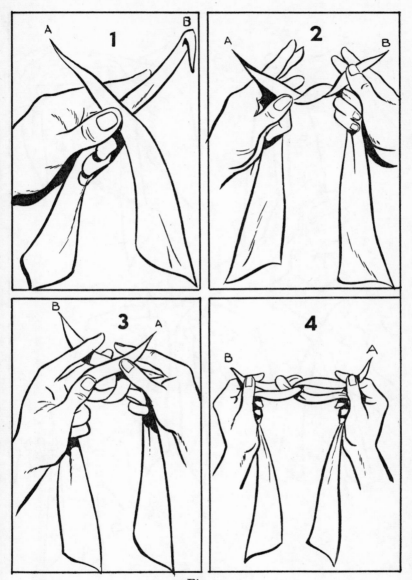

Fig. 33

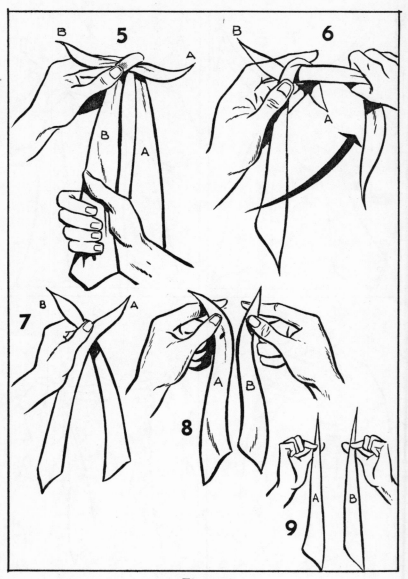

Fig. 34

it out from behind end A, partially untwisting the pseudo-knot.

Note: Handkerchief B will be twisted slightly, as a result of the tying process, so as you raise it to the right, the hand should rotate the handkerchief counter-clockwise. This will remove the twists.

Allow handkerchief B to drop, making sure it drops past A on the side toward you. Grasp A and raise it as shown in #7. The audience thinks there is still a double knot held by the left thumb and fingers. Actually, end A is merely crossed over end B.

The right thumb and fingers hold B at the point of crossing, while the left thumb and fingers retain their grip on A. Twist the ends upright as in #8, so the two handkerchiefs are side by side, without the slightest turn in either of them.

Pause at this point for several seconds. In the silence that results, snap the nail of one thumb on the nail of the other. Immediately following this click, bring the hands slowly apart, the palms opened toward the audience (#9). The handkerchiefs should be at the extreme tips of each thumb and forefinger, so the audience can see there are no twists in the cloth.

Note: The trick can also be done with the diagonally opposite corners of a single handkerchief. Before crossing the ends, it is a good idea to hold the handkerchief by one end and twist it by moving the hand rapidly in a clockwise motion. This twisted end becomes B when the ends are crossed. As you perform the trick, the moves automatically unwind this end and you will finish with an untwisted handkerchief.

KNOTS [*Tony Slydini*]

You need only a four-foot length of rope for this trick. Fig. 35, #1, shows the only preparation. Taking the rope by the ends, have the spectators see you make the knot in the center of the rope. Next knot the two ends together as shown in #1.

In an old version of this trick the performer explained that under these conditions there was no possible way to get the knot in the center of the rope, off the rope. The solution was to put the rope behind your back and run the knot up the rope so that it joined the knotted ends. You then hoped that no one would notice that the knot at the ends had become bigger. Do this, and if your audience doesn't notice the increase in the size of the knot you can explain it as you open up the little knot and bring it down to the center of the rope again as in #1.

Explain that this is the only way to do the effect—that is, by cheating a little, unless you pass the rope through the fourth dimension. To prove your boast, have a spectator hold the knotted ends of the rope below the knot so that he will feel it if you run the lower knot up into the top knot.

Have the spectator turn around and hold the rope behind him so that his body screens what you are doing. As soon as you are screened pull the lower knot as tight as you can into the soft rope at a point about six inches away from the hanging center of the rope (#2). With soft rope you can pull the knot so tight it is of smaller diameter than the rope itself. The position of the spectator's hand at the top is as in #2.

Once this has been done, the real work is done. The rest is bluff. Holding the tight little knot hidden behind the crotch of your thumb and forefinger, make a tangle of the rope (#3). The spectator will still hold the knotted ends right up till you have the tangle secure enough to hold momentarily. At this point ask the spectator to release his hold and bring the rope into view of the audience as shown in #3.

Look at the tangle as though you had failed. Shake the rope down till it hangs between your hands. The knot has vanished!

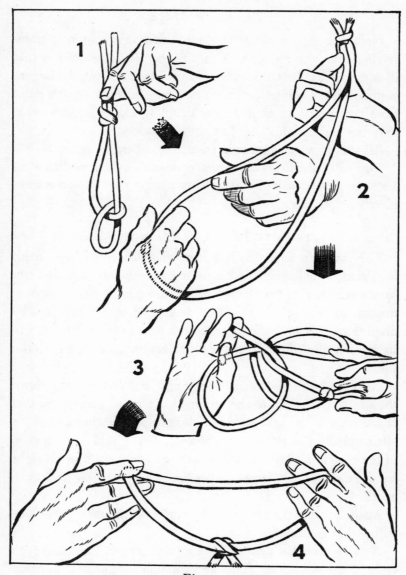

Fig. 35

Next rotate your hands to the position shown in #4, transferring your grip on the tiny knot to the position shown in that illustration #4. It is hidden behind your fore and middle finger; your hands are relaxed; there is no sign of a knot. At this point have the spectators examine the dangling knotted end so that they can see that this knot has not been added to.

All the drawings are made from the audience's view.

You will have to try this stunt on an audience to realize what a stunning effect it is. To all intents and purposes it seems completely impossible.

TEAR IT [*John P. Hamilton*]

The magician enters with a three foot length of rope in his left hand, doubled up. In his right hand he carries a blue silk handkerchief. Explaining that magic on occasion can solve non-magical problems, he proceeds. He creates such a problem by draping the silk over the center of the rope in his left hand. He then ties a single knot in the rope, thus tying the rope onto the silk.

Next he holds the rope by one end and lets it hang down showing the silk tied to the center of the rope. Taking the end of the rope in his right hand, he also grasps the other end in his left hand and slowly tightens the knot. Then, holding both ends of the rope in his left hand and both ends of the silk in his right hand, he shows how securely they are tied by yanking with each hand.

Again holding the rope aloft by one end, the silk is seen to be still tied in the center.

Now he takes both ends of the rope in his left hand and both ends of the silk in his right and mumbles, "Canasta, Canasta, Double Canasta!" He tugs on the silk and rope and a snap is heard. The silk is free of the rope in his right hand with a little piece of rope still tied around its center and his right hand now holds the rope in one solid piece. Clearly, the silk and the knot came right off the rope.

Tie a piece of thin elastic band around a loop of the length of the rope as shown in Fig. 36, #1. You will have to be careful not to tie it too tightly, or too loosely.

Pretending to tie a knot in the rope as in #2 by twisting the ends slightly as you apparently pull the knot tight will help to keep the loop in the rope. As you pull on the ends, instead of a knot you are left with an unknotted length of rope with a small piece of elastic around its center. This is, of course, the principle upon which the trick is based.

Take an eighteen inch silk handkerchief and tie a piece of rope around it as shown in #3. Making a single knot, trim the ends as short as you can. Then, twist the ends of the silk around the knot, hiding it. Take a pencil and use its point to tuck in the ends of the silk, thus securing them.

Hold the rope as in #1 (your thumb and forefinger hiding the elastic) in your left hand. Show the silk in the right hand and place it over the rope as in #4. Pretend to tie a knot in the rope. As you pull the ends of the rope, the elastic will slip down and hold the silk on the rope. It will seem to be really tied in place. You can now take both ends of the rope in your left hand and both ends of the silk in your right and tug away.

To cause the miracle to take place, contrive to get both ends of the silk outside the loop as shown in #6. Don't expose this side to the viewers. However, the view they get is of the other side as in #5. The silk appears to be looped over the rope and tied in place.

Take both ends of the rope in your left hand and both ends of the silk in your right. Pull your hands apart. The elastic will break, making an audible snap. This releases the silk from the

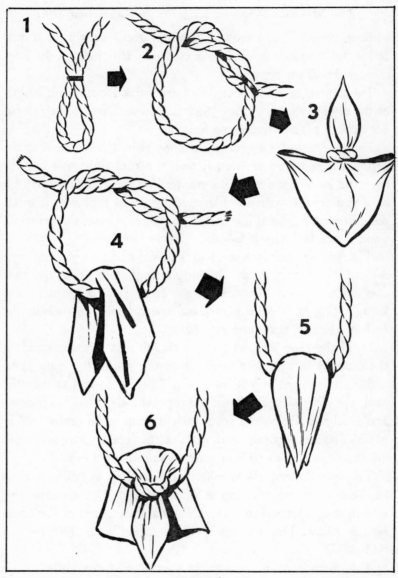

Fig. 36

rope. The spectators see the rope in its entirety and unknotted in your left hand and the silk in your right hand with the little bit of rope still knotted around its center!

CAUGHT KNOT [*John A. M. Howie*]

This is a brief interlude with a piece of rope which may well introduce a routine of knots. Required is a rope some four feet long with a plain knot tied about ten inches from one end. Show the rope and pass it from hand to hand keeping the knot hidden all the time. Eventually position the rope as shown in Fig.37, #1, the knot being hidden by the left hand. At this point you are standing directly facing the audience.

Turn left so your right side is toward the audience. As you start to turn, the hands come together momentarily as in #2. Note that the right first and second fingers grip the rope just above the hidden knot while the left fingers grip the other end of the rope at the back of the right fingers. The left hand remains low while the right hand moves upwards till the right forearm is quite vertical. This procedure puts an "instantaneous knot" on the rope near the middle, this knot being hidden by the right arm as in #3.

Flick the upper end of the rope (X) over the back of the right hand, point upward with the right forefinger, and then give the whole rope a vigorous flick upward. Apparently you succeed in flicking the rope in such a way as to produce a knot (#4).

Using the left hand, untie the knot and state your intention of trying again. This time the effect is produced by switching the end held in the hand (X) for the other end (Y). To do this, swing the rope outward then jerk it so that the end (Y) flicks back toward the right hand. As this happens, strike the right hand downward, release the knotted end (X), and seize the other end (Y). Done rapidly, it appears that you have

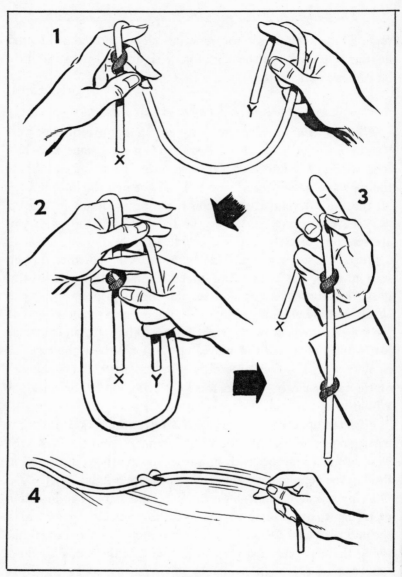

Fig. 37

merely given the rope another vigorous flick to produce another knot.

NOT AT ALL [*Dr. Wiener*]

The difference in this rope trick is that at the point in most rope effects where the magician says, "Let's cut the rope in the middle," and then cuts it at one end, in this method the audience *sees* that he is cutting it in the middle. What's more, not only is the rope cut in the middle, it is cut twice, once on each side of an identifying knot tied in the middle of the rope by the magician in full view of the spectators.

When the hocus pocus is applied, the rope and the knot are restored.

Your only preparation is to tie a knot in the end of the rope near one of the ends (Fig. 38, #1). This knot is hidden in the left hand as shown at point X in #2, while the magician visibly ties a knot in the exact center of the rope at point Y. Not much preparation, is it?

The rope-cut itself is one that is generally used for the cut-and-restored-turban. This is the one where you exchange the middle of the rope for one end in the action of picking up a pair of scissors with which to cut the rope.

The illustrations show the method. The hands are held as in #3. The extra knot is hidden by the left thumb. Fig. 39, #4, shows the beginning of the transfer of the real middle of the rope for the left hand end.

Your hands are in this position when you reach for the scissors which are on the table to your left. As your hands go down for the scissors, your left ring and little fingers take the real middle of the rope while your left fingers allow the right hand middle ring and little fingers to grasp the left end of rope as shown in #5.

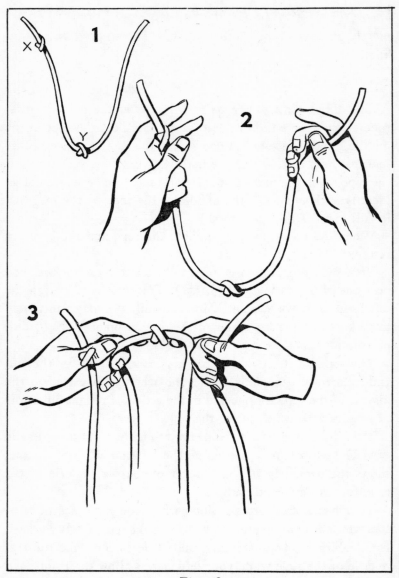

Fig. 38

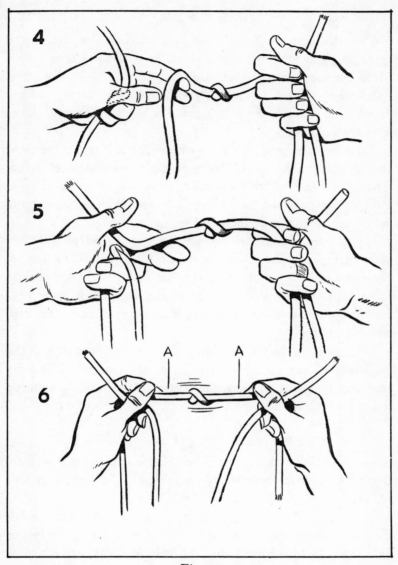

Fig. 39

Close the fingers of both hands, concealing the fact of the exchange, and everything looks just as it did a moment ago. Hold out the rope to be cut as in #6.

Ask the spectator to cut the knot out of the "center" of the "rope". He cuts at point A-A in #6. He holds this up and shows it to the audience.

Take the knot back from the spectator, hold it under the right thumb, and proceed to roll the rope itself around the left hand. The right hand conceals the knot in the cut-off piece of rope. Roll the rope around the left hand starting from the center, not at one of the ends as in the usual rope cuts.

Go to your pocket with the scissors, getting rid of the extra piece of rope, or simply retain it in the right hand as you let the restored rope unroll from the left hand. A double miracle takes place simultaneously as far as the audience is concerned, for the rope restores itself and the knot appears back in the center of the rope!

When you tie the visible knot in the middle of the rope at the beginning of the effect, don't make a big thing of it, just say that you are going to mark the center of the rope by knotting it and let it go at that.

CUT TO MEASURE [*Walter Gibson*]

Here is a "cut and restored" effect that is as novel as it is effective. What is more, its novelty includes, of all things, a dash of logic!

It's a trick of the convincing type wherein the item used is measured before and after, but the item isn't a string, a rope, or an alleged turban. Since something is to be measured, it's quite logical that the magician should use a tape measure, and having such a thing to hand, why should he bother with anything else?

A paper tape measure is used, the kind that can be bought for a few cents (Fig. 40, #1). You need a gimmick to go with it but this is cheap, too, for it is merely a 4 or 6 inch piece cut from another paper tape measure. Assume you're using a tape measure one yard long and are going to cut it right in the middle.

To prepare, first fold the measure across the 18 inch mark. Next, from the other measure, cut a piece 4 inches long, from the 16 inch mark to the 20. Crease this across the center too, but if the tape is creased *outward* the fake must be creased *inward*, as shown in #4.

The fake is attached neatly to the center of the measure, that is, from inches 16 to 20. The fake should be gummed very slightly, just at the ends. A mere dab of paste or mucilage will suffice.

You now have what looks like an ordinary tape measure except for a double thickness at the center which has a tendency to open diamond-fashion, if you let it—which you don't, not yet. Instead, you will find that if you have pasted the short strip accurately, you can draw the tape measure through your fingers inch by inch, close to the eyes of the observers right past the fake, without anyone noticing it at all.

Drawn taut, the fake flattens out against the tape measure and the only possible give-away could be the cut-off ends but you've hidden them by cutting along the inch marks, 16 and 20, which hide the edges perfectly. Moreover, all the while you draw the tape measure through your hands you are calling attention to the empty condition of the latter. Seemingly you have nothing but a paper tape measure of the most ordinary pattern.

Turn the tape over and run it through your fingers again in order to find the exact center, which can't be missed on a tape measure. At this time the fake strip is uppermost and you don't have to look for it because the inch marks themselves will tell

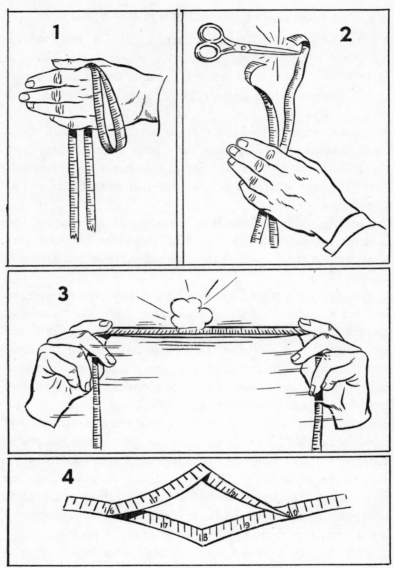

Fig. 40

you when you reach it. Stop with the center of the tape stretched from one hand to the other, the backs of your hands to the audience. Hold the tape taut with one thumb and forefinger at the 16 inch mark—the other thumb and forefinger at the 20 inch mark.

Now for a simple and deceptive move. Simply push the hands together extending your fingers as you do. The *fake* center of the fake pops *upward* because of its crease and the real center goes *down* because of its opposite crease. The fingers hide the manoeuvre and the spectators see the center all the time, never realizing that the tape has "split" into two central portions (#2).

The left hand grips the tape alone and there you are—holding a tape measure that you have legitimately folded in half, with the 18 inch mark proclaiming the fact. Down in your hand is the real center, with the fake part on display.

Reaching for a pair of scissors, the right hand proceeds to cut the center off the tape. Not only that, it trims away the fake close to the 16 and 20 inch marks that are between the thumb and forefinger of the left hand. Since this whole section is to be restored, it is suggested that the clippings be dropped into an ash tray that has a piece of tissue paper, preferably flash, ready to receive the clips. Paper and clippings are burned by the right hand, which sprinkles a few ashes on the stumps of the tape measure still held by the left hand.

Then with both hands working together, the center of the tape is drawn taut with hands turning inward to cover the "pop up" of the real center.

This rubbing restoration enables the fingers to draw away any remnants of the gummed fake ends. The tape measure is then stretched to full length and placed in the hands of the spectators. Bringing the hands together to get rid of ashes disposes of any tiny paper remnants.

Another suggestion: In doing the trick, the tape measure can be cut *twice*, each a foot apart. This simply means two fakes, one at the 12 inch mark and another at the 24. You poke one up from the left hand—then run along to the other and poke it up beside the first. Both should be cut and ash-sprinkled at the same time, but restored separately by drawing the tape out with the right hand, the left hand merely aiding with its fingers. This should really confound the skeptics.

CHAPTER 4

♥ ♣ ♦ ♠

Card Tricks that Work Themselves

Without exception the sterling effects in this chapter need no skill. The magic, so to speak, is built into them, incorporated by the cleverness of the inventors.

Since there is no skill required on your part, you can concentrate on presentation, on the smoothness of your actions and the cleverness of your patter.

PAY-OFF [*Walter Gibson*]

This is an idea that has been simmering for years, waiting only for the touch that would turn it into a real baffler. The answer was found recently making this as capital an impromptu mystery as has ever seen the light.

Asking the spectator to shuffle an ordinary pack of cards, you have him cut it into two heaps, fairly close in size. Since he is going to guess the colors without looking at the faces, you give him the smaller heap so the process will take less time. Tell him to deal his cards one by one, calling aloud "red" or "black" with each card dealt, just as may occur to him.

When he has finished and gathered up his heap, shake your head and tell him he was way off. "For instance," you say, "you went far too heavy on the reds. Why, my heap has four more reds than yours has blacks!" Or, you may say it this way, "Why, I have four more reds than you have blacks."

You have meanwhile picked up the heap and, to prove your statement, you count its red cards while he counts the black cards in his. To his amazement, you are right. It turns out that you have, for example, 14 reds while he has only 10 blacks.

Now comes the remarkable sequel. Exchanging heaps, you each proceed to shuffle your cards separately, so there can be no telling the rotation of reds and blacks in each. To make it even fairer, you do nothing except extend your heap and have him deal on some cards from his, calling "red" or "black" with each card dealt.

Again you shake your head and tell the spectator, "You only *guessed*, whereas I *know*. Almost all the cards you gave me were blacks. Why, I now have three more blacks than you have reds!" To prove this, you count the blacks in your heap while he counts the reds in his. Right again! For instance, you now have 12 blacks while he has only 9 reds.

All you have to know is the number of cards in each heap. You learn this very subtly while the spectator is dealing his cards and guessing "red" and "black." Thus engrossed, he doesn't count his cards when he deals them—but you do.

Your balance number is 26. If he deals 22 cards, he is 4 under that number and you are therefore 4 cards over, which means you will have 4 more reds than he has blacks. It also happens that you will have 4 more *blacks* than he has *reds* so that you can state the proposition either way. However, you only state it one way, giving the impression that while he was *guessing* colors, you were *telling* them.

The sequel is equally important. The reason you exchange heaps is so that when he deals cards from his to yours, he will be building up the smaller heap into the larger, again giving you the favorable balance. Suppose from the pile of 30 cards you give him, he deals 7 onto the 22 that you hold.

Subtract *4* (the previous difference) from *7* (the number dealt) and you have *3*, which is the new difference. So now you have *3 more* blacks than he has reds. Oddly enough, you like-wise have 3 more *reds* than he has *blacks*, so you can put it vice versa, if you wish. The best system is to state it one way the first time, the other way the next. Just follow the method given and the cards do the rest!

Remember only this: Whatever your margin over 26—you will have that many more of one color than he has of the other. By exchanging heaps before he shuffles and deals more cards to you, a smaller heap is built up to a larger, thus giving a new result through subtraction instead of addition.

This is the point that sells the sequel. Adding cards to the larger heap would produce too great a difference. The other way about, the whole thing is kept within bounds, and since no one knows that you are working from the balance number, 26, the mystery is complete.

Naturally, the joker is discarded before beginning the trick. You can use a pinochle deck, in which case the balance number is 24. Or the trick can be varied by using less than a full pack, provided that reds and blacks are first discarded equally. Your balance number, in any case is simply half of the total cards used.

TOPPER [*Walter Gibson*]

The effect of this card trick affords the best preliminary to its explanation. A spectator is told to think of a number under twenty and to deal off that many cards. He is then to divide the rest of the pack into two heaps, shuffling each separately. Picking up the dealt cards, he notes the one on the bottom of the packet, and places it between the other heaps. The whole pack is then shuffled.

Glancing through the deck, the performer asks someone to

name *another* number aloud. Dealing to that number, he asks the name of the card first chosen and turning up the card to which he has just dealt, it proves to be the same card.

This trick has an odd solution. Probably every magician has noticed that if a spectator deals cards onto the table one by one, reversing their order, people generally believe that the bottom card of such a group represents the final number, and *not* the top card of the pack.

In fact, several counting and spelling tricks take advantage of this mental lapse, but the reverse deal has always seemed too bold unless the right system is employed, and this trick provides it.

The magician knows the top card of the pack, sighting it, or getting it there by a simple shuffle. Handing the pack to his victim, he emphasizes the choice of a number, demonstrating or indicating that the cards are to be dealt silently, one by one. That done, the misdirection enters.

All attention is taken from the dealt cards by telling the spectator to divide the pack and shuffle the halves separately, then to pick up his heap, square it, and note the card on the bottom. Add here, that he is *not* to forget his number—and the cause is won.

His attention having been drawn away, the spectator will forget how he dealt the cards (if he thought of it at all) and take it for granted that the card he looked at was the one dealt from his number. When the magician gives the word to shuffle the entire pack, people will begin to wonder. When he looks for the card and doesn't find it, his asking for *another* number further settles the issue, by marking the trick as a failure.

However, having forced the card, the magician simply counts from it toward the top, while, spreading the cards and dividing the pack at that point, he counts down and completes the surprising coincidence. By then, the subterfuge on which the trick depends is so far in the past as to be totally forgotten.

ONE GOOD TRICK DESERVES ANOTHER
[*Walter Gibson*]

For a clean, baffling effect, the original "Card in Pocket" mystery is hard to surpass.

In effect, a person shuffles a deck, notes any card and its number from the top. Receiving the pack, the magician riffles it behind his back, removes a card, and pockets it. Said card proves to be the chosen one.

Simply remove the *top card* and pocket it without showing the face. Ask for the chosen *number* so you can count down to it. In counting, draw cards off with the right thumb, letting each card fall on the one before it, in the right hand, thus reversing the order of the cards.

At the spectator's number, thumb the card directly from the pack to the table with left hand. The card goes face down and while the spectator is turning it over to find it is not his, you replace the right hand packet on the deck, palm the top card, reach in your pocket and bring it out as the one originally in the pocket.

It proves to be the chosen card! The misdirection is perfect and you simply leave the extra card in your pocket—unless a wise spectator tried to cross you by remembering the top card of the pack, in which case, you already have his card. *And now—*

Shuffle to a fare-you-well, a borrowed pack is handed to the magician, who riffles the cards while a spectator is *thinking* of any number from 1 to 52.

Laying the pack aside, the magician writes something on a slip which he folds and gives to a spectator. Asking the chosen number, the magician counts down to it, dealing the cards on the table one by one, very fairly.

Arrived at the chosen number, the performer pockets the card without looking at it. The slip is opened; on it is found the name of a card. Bringing out the card he pocketed, the magician —like the spectators—is amazed to find it the very card predicted.

This "Pocket Prediction" is the sequel to the "Card in Pocket" described before. In doing that first trick, you note and remember the "extra" card which you first put in your pocket and let remain there. You write the name of *that card* on your slip.

Deal to the newly chosen number. In pocketing the card at that number, palm it. Simply bring hand from pocket, gather the dealt cards and add them to the pack, the palmed card with them.

The name of the card is read from the slip. From the pocket you bring out that very card—the *only* card now in your pocket. Apparently you predicted the card at the exact number mentally chosen by your victim.

IT GOES DOUBLE [*Ted Annemann*]

Dating back before Professor Hoffmann's period, this trick drifted into oblivion, only to pop up some twenty years ago as a "fooler" that had even magicians guessing. So simple that it seemed awful, the thing dazed all witnesses because of its sheer audacity, plus the fact that its ancient originator had a marvelous eye for misdirection.

The effect is straightforward—and repeated. The magician cuts the pack into two heaps and declares that by looking at the top card of one heap, he can name the top card of the other. He glances at the top card of the heap near him, without showing it and replaces it, saying, "The card *here* tells me that the one *there* is the six of spades." Openly turning up the top card of the far heap, it proves to be the six of spades.

Completing the cut, the magician turns the pack around and again lifts off half. Glancing at the top card of the near heap, he "learns" that the top card of the far heap is the queen of spades—which it proves to be. Another gather of the pack, a cut into two piles, and another card is named in the same fashion. And so on—and on, as long as the magician wishes.

The secret is that the *far* heap is the top half of the pack. First, the magician notes the top card, by a peek, or shuffle of the bottom card to top. Cutting the pack away from him, he looks at the top card of the near half and pretends that *it* tells him the top card of the far heap, a card he already knows.

Now in completing the cut, the magician puts the near heap on the far one and in so doing, knows the *new* top card, because it is the one he so casually glanced at in order to "name" the other! Every repeat is just the same. The magician is naming one card by what seems pure hokum and in so doing is setting up for the next time.

Don't reject this until you've tried it. It's casual, rapid, and more perplexing as it goes along. Turning the pack around with each gather is helpful byplay and an occasional riffle shuffle thrown in (keeping the top card in position) is also effective, though once or twice in a dozen "namings" is sufficient.

All the trick ever lacked was a finish. It wound up only when the magician wanted to quit. This is where the Annemann improvement entered, one of those subtle ideas that really make a trick. When he showed it as a pay-off—you had to start thinking all over again.

Here is the Annemann finish. After numerous requests, the magician suddenly says that the glance at one card isn't necessary. He can name the top cards of *both* heaps just as readily as one—and without reference to any other card. He then names the top cards of both heaps, near and far, tossing them both face upward, showing that he has correctly called them!

It is the same neat misdirection with a twist. Ready for the pay-off, the magician actually knows *one* card, the top card of the pack, which is on the far heap—say the three of spades. Stating that he can name the top cards of both heaps, he points to the heap near his right hand and calls, "Three of spades." With that, he lifts the card, *face toward him*, transferring it from right hand to left. Glimpsing it without even a noticeable glance, he notes it—say the nine of hearts.

Then, without an instant's hesitation, he points to the top card of the far heap and calls, "Nine of hearts," promptly picking up that card, *face toward him*, with the right hand. As he carries the card toward himself, the left hand moves forward with its card, *past* the card in right hand, thus coming in front of it. The right hand simply clips both cards and drops them faces up.

It's not a special move. It's merely a transfer done as naturally as the pick-ups. But when the cards fall, the three of spades is seen *above* the nine of hearts. That is, the cards are laying in the order as called, though no mention is made of the fact. Thus the trick reaches its double-barreled finish—a perfect pay-off, Annemann style.

One subtle twist having supplanted another, the spectators are not only baffled by the climax, but thrown completely off the first track of the trick!

21 PLUS [*Shaman*]

Here's the good old "Twenty-One" trick really streamlined, as you'll learn when you try it. From a shuffled pack deal 3 batches of 7 cards each, faces down. Have a spectator pick up any heap, note a card in it and place the heap between the other 2.

Now deal 3 rows of cards, still faces down. Have the person guess which heap his card is in and then look to see if he's right. If he says it's there, you compliment him. If it isn't, give him another try. This byplay enables you to learn which heap the card is in and again it goes between the other two heaps.

Another deal of 3 rows. Let him guess if he wants, but it doesn't matter. The idea is that he is to give you whatever heap his card is in, so you can show something better than guesswork. You receive the heap face down. You haven't seen the face of any card.

Now the pay-off. Simply spell the cards in the heap, shifting one from top to bottom with each letter: "T-H-I-S I-S T-H-E C-A-R-D Y-O-U T-O-O-K." At the end of each *word*, pronounce the word and toss away the top card. After "took" you have just one card left. So you say, "This is the card you took," and you turn it face up. It is!

DISCARD [*Jack Miller*]

This is a real lazy man's stunt. The directions are clear, and it can be done both in person and over the telephone.

The spectator is directed to lay out two even rows of cards. The performer has no idea how many cards there are because if you do it in person you have your back turned and, if on the telephone, obviously you don't know. By even rows is meant that if 4 cards are placed in the top row, 4 are placed in the second row. If 5 go on top, 5 go on the bottom. The numbers matter not at all, as long as both rows are equal.

Direct the spectator to discard one card from the bottom row. Next, ask—and it's your only question—how many he wants to discard from the top row. Remember whatever number is given. Let's say it is 3.

Next, tell the spectator to take from the bottom row as many as are left on the top row and discard this bunch. That is, the bunch from the bottom row.

Finally, they are to discard the remainder of the top row. The answer, and it is an eye-popper, is that you tell them how many cards are left. There does not seem to be any way you can know that there are, in this instance, 2 cards left. The answer must always be one less that the number called out. In this case it was 3—so 2 is the eye-popper. Try this on the phone; it's worth the dime!

DOUBLE STOP [*Franklin V. Taylor*]

The effect of this trick is spectacular as a trial will show you. It is also efficient, since with only a modicum of trouble you are able to find two freely chosen cards, identifying one of them, and then so place both of them that when two packets are dealt out the chosen cards appear simultaneously.

The method uses one of the most primitive devices known to magic, namely, a red-black separation of the deck—26 blacks and 26 reds. Having separated the cards this way you next make your set-up which is not complicated. It is: 20 reds on top of the deck, 26 black, and then the other 6 red cards on the bottom. That's all. The rest is in the handling.

Assume that you have a deck so arranged. Place it on the table. Have spectator A cut off a small packet of about eight or ten cards from the top of the deck. He is then to cut off a similar packet from the bottom of the deck. He retains his hold on the center packet of cards that is left. You point out that after these cuts there is no earthly way you can know the identity of the top or bottom card in the packet he holds. (This is true.) He is to look at the top card of the packet in his hand and remember it. Next he is allowed to cut his packet as often as he wants to and to hold on to it.

Turn to spectator B and ask him to pick up the packet that was cut off the bottom of the whole pack. He is to cut this packet as often as he wishes and then to remember the top card of this packet. He is not to cut this packet now (you don't say this) but is to pick up packets off the group which was cut off the top of the deck and drop them on the packet in his hand. He can make many little packets of this group and finally drop the remaining cards on top of his packet.

You then point out that you have not touched his cards at any time, which is true, and that you will not touch them at any time, which is also true and is one of the most baffling parts of the effect to an astute observer.

Turn to spectator A and ask him to think of his card. Take the packet from him and fan it in front of you, asking for his mental aid as you do so. As you fan the packet in front of you, find the first red card in the fan from the right hand side (from the face of the deck) and cut it to the face of the packet. Count the number of red cards and remember the last red card in the group and its number. It is the chosen card, but continue your count on into the black cards until you count to 20 and cut there, finishing the cut. Remember two things. The identity of the chosen red card and its number. Subtract its number in the fan from 20 and your work is over. Assume the last red card, the ten of diamonds, was the eighth card. Subtract this from 20 and remember 12.

Hand the pack back to spectator A and ask both spectators to deal cards simultaneously, one at a time, face down. They do so. You count with them while they deal and in this example you stop them when they have dealt 12 cards.

At 12 you say stop, so that their cards are the next ones on the packets.

You don't know the name of spectator B's card but you gloss over this and point out that there is no way you could have known how far down his card was. Have him name it and ask him to turn over the card after the twelfth. "Hola," you say, "the ace of hearts!"

Turn to spectator A. "I have read your mind! Your card is the ten of diamonds!" He turns it over and there is his card.

Handled this way, you will find that people forget that you didn't name both cards before they were turned over, so that the effect is completely impossible when they try to back-track. The fact that you know where to stop spectator A makes it seem as though you MUST know the identity of his card too.

It would be finicking to separate the deck into black odds and red evens and red odds and black evens, although a scrupulous worker might do so in order to make the effect even harder to reconstruct.

JOHN DOE—MAGICIAN [*Tommy Dowd*]

You demonstrate with a deck of cards how an ordinary magician fans a deck, has a card selected and returned to the deck, and finally locates it. Having done this, select a spectator and ask him to be the magician for a spectacular trick.

Have him fan the deck in front of you and take a card. You return it just the way your hapless victims do all the time. The spectator closes up and squares the deck. Ask him if there is any way he can find your card, the three of spades, without looking at the faces of the cards.

When he admits his inability, ask him to spell out the name of the card, a card at a time.

He does so and on the "S" finds himself staring at your card!

All you do is put the three of spades, or whatever card you desire, as deep down from the top of the deck as it has letters in its name. That's all. The card that you take from the spectator, you disregard and miscall as the three of spades. Too simple? Won't fool anyone? Try it!

YOU'RE A LIAR [*Paul Curry*]

This trick is accompanied by patter about the use of lie detectors. You maintain that you can tell when the spectator tells the truth and when he lies. You prove it, for when he miscalls his card you are able, because of the mechanics of the trick, to call him on his lie.

The method is simplicity itself. All you need do after shuffling a deck is note the bottom card, which you use as a key card. The spectator takes a card and you have it returned under the key card.

The effect proceeds with the spectator dealing off card after card from the deck, face down, naming the cards as he does so.

You press him to be sure that he does not change his facial expression or the tone of his voice when he comes to the card that he chose and which he is going to miscall.

Listen till he names the key card. You know the next card is his and when he names it, calling it by another card's name, you instantly tell him he is lying.

This is the basic effect and one which has proved itself through the years. Now try it with the Paul Curry addition and see how strong it is.

Curry has found that this is the most powerful trick he can do for a female audience. If you've wanted a card trick that would not put the distaff side to sleep, try this one.

The method is the same as the basic one. The handling is different in only one respect. Before you present the trick take a card (a file card is good) and write in bold block letters on the card: YOU'RE A LIAR!

Set it down on the table near you with the letters on your side. Crimp one narrow end of the card just enough so that you can balance it upright.

As you do this, be sure that the card is set so that when it falls down the letters will be arranged so the spectator can read them the instant the card falls.

Proceed with the basic trick until the spectator names the key card. When he miscalls the card, breathe out through your nostrils or out of the corner of your mouth so that you blow the card over.

There is a fine shocking effect to this. Just as the spectator lies, the card falls over and accuses him of what he has done. If you work for genteel people who may be offended by being called a liar, you can letter TCH, TCH! on the card, or OH, OH!

TIME MUST TELL [*Cy Endfield*]

There is a principle in card work known by few and used by fewer, with which it is possible to be a consistent worker of miracles. Using it properly, even on the initiate, seldom fails to leave a very puzzled spectator indeed. The principle involves the identification of a card from its back by means of "natural" markings. By "natural" I mean the spots, nicks, and oddments of dirt and abrasions or actual printing defects that any white bordered backed deck of cards will pick up after it has been used several times.

Admittedly, it takes keen eyes and a moments study to find these minute blemishes, but practice at this form of recognition brings improvement and speed.

To use this principle properly, provision (i.e., excuse) must be made for studying the back of the card after it is selected and during the location. But if the spectators, even magically trained ones, can be diverted from the notion that you are studying the backs excessively, they are bound to be deceived. The following trick is designed to take maximum advantage of this principle.

The spectator is using his own pack. After he shuffles it I turn my back and ask that he remove any card, look at it, and then place it face down on the table. I then turn around, take the deck and state that I will form a circle of 12 face-down cards, clock-wise, with the spectator's card at the twelve o'clock position. While doing this I have more than ample time to observe the selected card's unique blemishes.

Next, I turn my back again and ask that the spectator interchange his selected card with any other, remembering at what "o'clock" his card is now placed. I further ask that he interchange a number of the cards so that I can't determine where the selected card has been placed by any such simple method as observing its displacement.

When I turn back the following situation exists from the spectator's point of view. A card has been selected under completely uncontrolled conditions and hopelessly lost among eleven others, the name and position not conceivably known to the magician.

The patter ensuing will describe the action of the effect: "We've often heard the expression, 'Time must tell,' but the question is, just what will it tell? Working on the theory of fair exchange and considering how often I have 'told time,' I now ask time to tell me what card you have selected. Further, this will be without your cooperation. No matter what question I ask you, you will answer 'no,' and of course you must try to prevent me from knowing when the 'no' is a lie. For instance, I point to this card at four o'clock and ask you, 'Have you placed your card at four o'clock?' Whether or not you have, you answer 'no.' Let's proceed. Have you placed your card at seven o'clock [I point and the spectator answers 'no'] at nine, at two, at four?" (By thus continuing you ultimately come to the marks or recognition on the back of the selected card. Continue pointing to cards at other clock positions, perhaps insistently asking spectator if he has placed his card at ten o'clock, though you already know that it is at seven o'clock.)

"Well, the only thing that time has told me so far is that somewhere along the line you are not telling me the truth. So I proceed with my questioning, and again you say 'no' to any questions I ask. I turn up the card at two o'clock and ask if this queen of diamonds is your card? No? The four of spades? No? Of course, you must say 'no' to whatever I ask." (Continuing, I turn up each of the cards, naturally observing the name of the card at the position earlier identified. But even after they are turned up I go back to the cards, asking again and again if this or that one is the selected one. The spectator insistently answers in the negative. Finally I narrow the choice to the selected card and one other. Then, at last, I keep pointing to the selected card and one other. Finally, I keep pointing to the selected card, say a king of spades, and request over and over, "Is it this? Is it this?" and the most controlled spectator must break up as he realizes that you know his secret.)

"I admit," I say in conclusion, "that this stunt took quite a long time, but that was how I knew on which card you lied about the time and about the name. It was the time that told me."

HAND TO HAND [*Martin Gardner*]

This is as neat a two card revelation as could be demanded;

no skill, a befuddling presentation and an unusual ending. Here's how.

Any two cards are taken from a shuffled deck. Have them returned and shuffle them to the top. Riffle shuffle, retaining the two cards on top of the deck, and then overhand shuffle, sending the two cards to the bottom of the deck. Any lay audience will be convinced by this time that the cards are lost.

Cut the deck in the middle and reverse the top packet so that the deck is now half face-up and half face-down. Hold the deck in the left hand with the fingers on the bottom and the thumb on top. Let the deck fall from the left hand to the right, retaining the top and bottom cards in the left hand. This is simply done.

The deck is now in the right hand. Hold it as before and let the deck drop from right hand, left retaining the top and bottom cards in the right hand.

Really, the bottom cards in each hand are now the chosen cards. Continue letting the cards drop from hand to hand in a fairly sloppy fashion but continue to retain the chosen cards on the bottom.

The audience sees different cards each time you drop the deck from hand to hand. This assures them that all is as it should be. At any time ask the spectators to tell you to stop.

When they do, simply turn your hands over and there, staring at them, are the two chosen cards.

PARALLELS [*Roger Barkann*]

An impromptu card trick, this is sufficiently "close-up" for an audience of one, sufficiently showy for an audience of a hundred.

Performer borrows 2 sturdy books and 2 decks of cards. In other words, there is absolutely no preparation or set-up. A person with such a perfect reputation as to preclude screams of "Stooge!" after the miracle has been disclosed is given both decks and asked to shuffle them. While he is doing this the magician explains that the books are merely to act as stands for a few cards, then sets them on end, one in front of the other. Each book should be wide enough to hold two cards each, and heavy enough to stand on end. If possible, one should be a few inches taller than the other, so that the front book will not hide the back one. The guest selects the deck he will use and gives the magician the other one. The magician then selects a card from his deck—the first step—and without showing it to anyone, places it between the pages of the rear book, back to the audience. The same actions are repeated with a few "minor" variations, so that 2 cards will have been selected by each. When the faces of the magician's cards are disclosed, each is identical with the card in front of it.

Remember: 1. You picked your cards before the assistant did. 2. The cards never left the sight of the audience. 3. You never touched the cards once they were chosen.

In order to create the illusion you have caused the spectator to select cards identical to yours, you actually use two basic principles, the "one ahead" and a subtle "force."

After he has shuffled the decks, the assistant is allowed to spread his deck, face upward, on the table. After you have glimpsed his top card (e.g., three of hearts) help him spread the cards better, actually pushing a few cards over the top one, to avoid his noticing its identity. Fan your own deck and, while you put on your most mystifying stare, look into the victim's eyes and into the deck alternately. When you locate his top card—3H—remove it from the deck and place it, back toward the audience, in position in the rear book. Warning—be careful that the card doesn't slip down into the book or you might be accused of a "switch" later on. Do not mention the fact that you are putting the card on the left side. Simply call attention to the fact that you will not touch this card again. Now ask your assistant to think of any card in the deck. When he has made up his mind, he is to remove it. Place this card in position in the front book, face outward. In other words, you make it clear that his card is directly in front of yours. The only trouble is that it is most unlikely to be the same as yours—if it is, stop while the stopping is good!

Patter to the effect that he has done very well and that you will try again. Run through the fan until you locate the duplicate of the card he chose—ace of spades—and, as though you suddenly became inspired to make things more difficult, cut that card to the top and put down the deck. "Let's make it tough this time. I want you to think of any number between 1 and 52—pardon me, 1 and 51. Don't just think of a number. Think of the number of cards you would cut if you were to cut your deck."

Start to cut your deck two or three times as though you are not sure, but finally do so. Put the cut-off packet on the table and the balance of the deck on top of it, at right angles. "I know that I am leading with my chin. You may see that I have read your mind, and then double-cross me. Please don't do that." Have him cut his cards and cross them as you did. Don't forget that you are supposedly thinking of a quantity of cards, so carry on by leaning over and sighting the two decks.

"No-o, I am afraid I missed by a few cards. But let's go ahead anyway." Remove the top card of your lower half—AS—and put it, back outward, in position in the rear book. Then ask him to give you the card to which he cut (?) and place it, face outward, in position in the front book. Two books now hold two pairs of cards.

Reiterate: You chose your cards before he did. No one saw the faces of your cards. You never touched the cards after putting them in book. The cards were never out of sight. If you were to turn the undisclosed cards at this point, there would be a sad situation. They would not pair up. But if you turn the rear book around, not only are the cards turned face-outward, but their positions are reversed, thus letting the audience see 2 pairs of cards, not only alike, but also parallel.

YOU DO AS I DO [*John Scarne*]

Hand a red-backed deck to a spectator, keeping a blue-backed deck. This is after they have been shuffled by you. Explain that you are going to name a number first—and that only after you have called the number will you ask the spectator to call one— any number at random. Let's say you call out 16 and the spectator calls out 22.

Hand him your deck and ask him to count off onto the table the number of cards that you called out (16) and you take his deck and count off the number he called out (22). Once this is done there is only one further direction. He is to pick up the packet of 16 cards and, holding it in the dealing position, he is to deal off a card onto the table and then transfer the next card from the top of the packet to the bottom of the packet. He is to continue doing this until his packet is exhausted and he is left holding one card. You do the same thing with your packet.

Placing a card on the table and one under the packet in unison you are both soon left holding a card apiece. You both turn over your cards. They are identical! If he turns over the three of spades, so do you! And this despite the fact that you called out your number before he did and that his number was a free choice!

There are 5 basic key numbers for you to work with: 2-4-8-16-

32. But you can shunt them off the low ones as being too easy. So 8-16-32 are the ones to remember. Next comes your only mental work. When he calls out his number, in the example, 22, you subtract the *nearest lower key* number, in this case 16, from 22. This leaves 6. Double it. Remember the number 12.

Despite the fact that you have shuffled the packs you have set them up to the extent that the top card on each is the three of spades. You will have no trouble in retaining a single card on top of each deck in a riffle shuffle. If this daunts you, you can just take the decks from the cases with the top cards set the same way and skip the shuffle.

When the spectator deals off 16 cards from the deck onto the table, this places your card at the bottom of the 16 cards and all is well. Your job is almost as easy. The number the spectator called was 22, the number you are remembering is 12. Count off cards from your left hand onto your right from 1 to 12. This puts the necessary card 12 down. From 12 on, deal the next 10 cards, not on top of each other as you have been doing up to this point, but under the 12. This change in procedure comes at the same time that the spectator is busy with his counting so that not even the most astute will notice any difference in the handling.

That's all there is to it. When you have become used to the handling you can employ a variant that will drive anyone crazy by calling out a series of numbers yourself and allowing someone to pick your number from the series you call.

All this employs is a four card set-up on top of each deck, as the top card is the ace of spades, the second the two, the third the three, and the fourth the four. This means that you can call out for the top card, 8-16-32. For the second, cutting the top card to the bottom of the deck, 7-15-31. For the third, cutting 2 cards to the bottom of the deck, you can call out 6-14-30. For the fourth, with 3 cards cut to the bottom, you can call out 5-13-29.

Holding the deck in your hand ready for a cut, you can say, "You pick which of these numbers I am to use, 5, 6, 7, 8, 13, 14, 15, 16, 29, 30, 31, 32 . . ." And pause as though you could go on forever. Whatever number is called, make the necessary small adjustment. No adjustment is necessary in the other deck.

CARD CLIMAX [*Scarne*]

Using the same key number arrangement means you can use Scarne's principle for a new finale to any card trick where a card is selected and brought to the top of the deck. Let us say the spectator has chosen the nine of clubs and you have brought it to the top of the deck. Ask him to choose a number as you count 8 to 16 or 32. Whichever he calls, hand him the deck and ask him to count off that number. Then have him pick up the packet and go through the one-card-on-the-table, one-under-the-packet routine and at the end he will be left holding his selected card.

PHONE MIRACLE [*Scarne*]

Call a friend on the phone and ask him to get a deck and shuffle it. Your only preparation is to have next to you on the table a sheet of paper with the numbers 1 to 52 written in a column. You will also need a pencil. Tell your friend over the phone that you are thinking of a card. (Ask him to cut a packet of cards off the deck and to place the rest of the deck to one side.) You think, you say, that the card you are thinking of is in the packet he holds. To make sure, ask him to hold the packet in his hand, face down, and to deal off the cards, calling out their names to you.

When he does this, jot down next to your list of numbers

the names of the cards, as (1) 3 of C for three of clubs and so on. You do this as fast as he can call off the names of his cards.

When he is done tell him that all is well, your card is in the packet he holds. Ask him to pick up the packet face down in his hand.

In front of you on the list you see how many cards there are in the packet he holds. Say he has 20. Subtract 16, the nearest key number from 20 which gives you 4. Double it and you have 8. Look at your chart for the eighth card he called, assume it was the ten of clubs. Remember this. Now, over the phone tell him to put on card from his packet onto the deck on the table, and one under the packet, as in the previous versions of this trick. He is to tell you when he is left with one card.

Ask him to place the card to one side on the table face down and to push the deck to one side. This destroys any evidence of how many cards he has counted.

You are all set. Tell him you were thinking of one card. Tell him to turn it over. With it facing him you now tell him the name of the card, in this case the ten of clubs. If that doesn't amaze him, he's a believer in telepathy.

BEST PREDICTION [*Scarne*]

Have the spectator shuffle the deck while you say that you'll make a prediction. Start to write the name of any card on a piece of paper or a stiff business card. Pause and ask the spectator to name a number. When he does, say that you can't be sure if your prediction will be in his packet so you will make an alternate prediction. Pretend to write the name of another card, but really just scratch out the one you have already written.

If he calls out 18, subtract 16, the nearest key which leaves 2. Multiply it by 2 and you get 4. Remember this.

Say that to make doubly sure that your card is in his packet you'd like him to count out the 18 cards face up on the table. When he does so all you have to do is spot the name of the fourth card. Remember it and as he proceeds to count out his cards you have all the time in the world to write the name of the fourth card, the nine of clubs for example, on your paper under the ones you've scratched out.

You write this down under the pretense of scratching out the alternate card which you have predicted. You can throw this face down on the table long before he has finished counting out his cards. When he has counted them, have him pick up the packet, deal off on the table, and put one under the packet in his hand till his packet is exhausted.

He is left, in this hypothetical case, with the nine of clubs in his hand. Let him pick up the paper and turn it over and read it. You are covered all around since your prediction was seemingly done far in advance.

"X-DECK" [*Ed Marlo*]

The performer spreads a deck of cards on the table, flips them over, scoops them up, shuffles them, and then re-spreads them. Reaching into the spread he picks out a card, scoops up the deck, squares it up, and then makes an X in pencil on the margin of the card. A spectator replaces the face-down card in the deck of cards. The deck is shuffled and then is spread face-up on the table. Any spectator takes any card out of the face-up spread. The performer scoops up the spread, squares it up, shuffles it and spreads it backs up on the table so he can look for the card with the X on its back.

No such card shows in the spread. The spectator turns over the card that was chosen at random—and it has the X on it!

This is perfect use for old decks of cards. Your only preparation is to make a penciled X in the middle of the left hand margin of fifty of the cards. On one of the unmarked cards, place a pencil dot at the top, right and left, bottom corner of the card. This card is placed in the center of the deck. The other unmarked card is placed on top of the deck.

With the deck prepared this way you will find that you can Hindu Shuffle, retaining the unmarked card on top of the deck and flashing it from time to time, and you can spread the deck safely. As long as you make the spread from right to left, no X's will show.

The rest of the trick follows the effect given. That is, spread the deck on the table, scoop it up, shuffle it and then square it up. Thumb riffle down in the deck until you hit the pencil-dotted card and remove it from the deck. Then make an X on the side of the card in the same place your other X's have been made. Replace this card in the deck, with its X-ed side to the left. Spread the deck face-up and allow a spectator to point to any card. Slide this card out of the spread—push it to one side. Scoop up the deck, shuffle, square-up, and spread backs-up, so that the X's don't show. Pretend to be astonished because the marked card does not show, and then have the spectator turn over the card he selected.

Seemingly he has chosen the only marked card in the deck. The small bit of preparation "X Deck" takes will more than repay you when the spectator reacts to it.

CHAPTER 5
♥ ♣ ♦ ♠

Card Tricks that Require Some Skill

Now we come to the kind of card magic that is dearest to my heart—flourishes, subtle sleights, effects that achieve their merit by the cleverness of your handling. In no case does any trick or sleight to be described need great skill or long practice, yet these are tricks that can make your reputation as a skillful finger-flinger.

Many of the best brains of today's magic world have contributed some of their best magic to this section—Dai Vernon, Dr. Daley, Bill Simon, Dr. Franklin V. Taylor. Here is "pure" magic, performed with a borrowed deck, without duplicates or gimmicks.

THE ELLIOTT CONTROL

Down through the ages prestidigitators have grappled with the problem of controlling a selected card once it has been chosen and returned to the deck. The classic pass, the Hindu Shuffle, and a variety of other means have all been developed and are perfect for certain people and certain occasions.

But each person works out a method that suits him best. Here is a way of controlling a card returned to the middle of the deck I have devised which I have found to be both clean and convincing.

Refer to Fig. 41, #1. The ace of diamonds has been selected

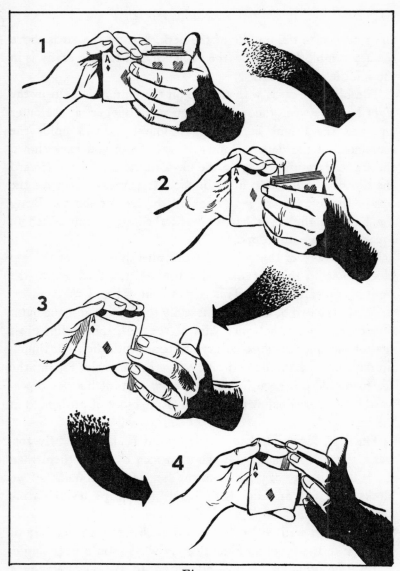

Fig. 41

and returned to the middle of the deck. Lift off the cards above the ace in a block and show the audience that the ace really is in the middle of the deck.

The block of cards with the ace on the bottom is held in the right hand between the middle joints of the fingers at the outer end and the thumb at the inner. The left hand holds the remainder of the deck as shown in #1. Once you have shown the ace to the audience, bring the block in the right hand toward the block in the left hand as in #2. As you do this press the tips of the left fingers *gently* against the face of the ace. Bring the block in the right hand toward the left thumb crotch to square up the entire deck.

The pressure of the left finger tips plus the action of the top block going to the left will push the selected card out to the right about half an inch. This is shown in #1 and #2.

Before the two blocks are completely squared against the outer tip of the ace by the inner part of the right pinky tip, press against the inner diagonal corner of the ace with the right thumb tip. Squeeze the thumb and pinky together slightly, forcing the ace to buckle downward as shown in #3. As it buckles downward it will curve below the bottom of the block of cards held in the left hand.

The left, lower block of cards should be held slightly forward, towards the audience, about an inch closer to them than the bottom block (#3). Extend the left fingers around the two blocks of cards and use both hands to square up the deck (#4).

The chosen card will have been brought from the middle of the deck to the bottom of the deck in what should be a single, graceful, continuous motion appearing to the audience as a simple squaring-up action.

If unacquainted with card stratagems, use this method of card control for any of the card tricks in this book that require you to bring a card to the bottom of the deck.

A LESSON IN MAGIC

I have always been intrigued with Nate Leipzig's spin pass. Any time you see card expert John Scarne with a deck of cards in his hands, you may be sure at one point or another he will do the spin pass which, by the way, is an error in nomenclature, since this move is not a pass but simply a flourish cut.

Having done the cut for ages and seen that the reason Scarne uses it so much, is that it can, on occasion, be used for everything from a peek, to a false cut—I then stumbled on something that to the best of my knowledge, is a completely new use for this pleasant little bit of handling. The magician, having baffled the laity to a fare-thee-well with a series of card locations, makes the offer magicians so love to make. He says, "Perhaps you'd be interested in learning precisely how a magician follows a selected card in its peregrinations through the deck."

Holding the deck in his right hand, he allows packets to fall from the right hand into the left, asking the audience to say "stop" at any point. Whenever they say "stop" he stops, and cuts the deck at the point indicated.

Double-lifting the top card(s) off the top of the deck, he says, "A random card, randomly chosen." He replaces the double lifted card(s) on top of the deck and picking off the real top card, face down, inserts it about halfway into the deck, and leaves an edge of the card protruding as he says, "Now a good magician, with a trained eye, would be able to gauge just how many cards down in the deck that selected card is."

The magician then does a simple, overhand shuffle, bringing the real top selected card down to the bottom of the deck as he says, "But now during the course of this shuffle, the card is, to all intents and purposes, lost in the mass of 51 other cards. Correct?" The audience will have to admit grudgingly that such is apparently the case.

"However," the magician says, "a very acute magician might well be able to determine where the wandering card is now. Therefore," the magician riffle shuffles the deck, but retains the selected card on the bottom of the deck. ". . . I'll riffle the deck. Certainly the card is now as lost as Ninevah and Tyre."

Given that the audience does not know about the existence of the double-lift and that they think the selected card originally went into the center of the deck, they are convinced the card is well and completely lost.

Enter the spin pass and its curious use for this effect.

The magician has the pack lying on his left palm, held loosely. Anyone who might suspect such chicanery as crimps, breaks and the like, should now be nonplussed.

Picking up the pack with the right middle finger at the far end and the right thumb at the near end, the magician runs his left thumb along the left side of the deck, saying, "As you can see, there is absolutely no physical clue by which the magician can determine precisely where the card is."

Pressing the inner edge of the left forefinger against the inner edge of the deck, the magician rotates a center packet out of the deck (Fig. 42, #1). The far end of the packet pivots on the grip the right, middle finger has on the far end of the deck (#2).

This middle packet is rotated all the way and is allowed to drop into the left palm; the right hand now holds the remainder of the deck with the bottom packet that has been withdrawn (#3).

The chosen card is still on the bottom of the deck in the right hand. The right hand comes closer to the waiting left

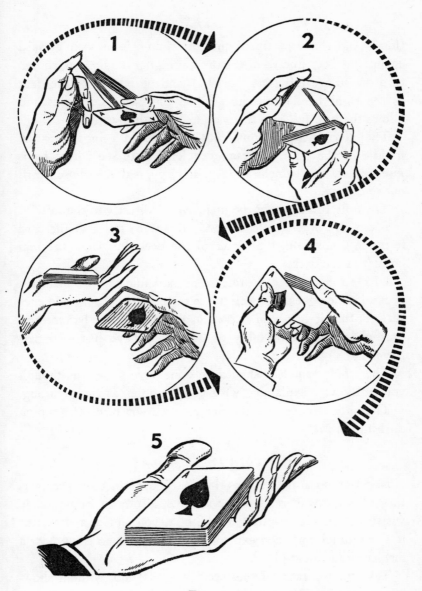

Fig. 42

thumb and the very tip of the left thumb is pressed upward against the bottom card of the deck, bringing the bottom, chosen card out to the left (#4), around, and up on top of the deck as the right hand drops its grip on the packets it holds and allows them to fall into the waiting left palm, #5.

The effect is that the magician has inserted a finger into the middle of the deck, without even looking to see where he is inserting it, and somehow, magically, popped the chosen card out into view.

The only bad angle in the maneuver is directly to the left.

From any other angle there is no way to tell that the card is coming, not from the center of the deck, but from the real bottom of the deck.

I have found that the pretense of explaining how a magician does a location goes over well, up to the point where the audience realizes that it has been tricked again. Then they become impressed by the impossibility of what they have just seen performed.

The whole sequence should be done very slowly as though you really were explaining what you are doing as you go along.

The only fast move is the finale, when you bring the chosen card into view.

B. D. V. [*Dai Vernon*]

Based on an almost self-working strip-out move of Vernon's, this, like so many really basic sleights, allows of innumerable variations. In the handling I like best, you shuffle a deck, cut it a few times and then explain that you'd like to show how a magician can win at poker.

Take the top card off the face-down deck and, without showing its identity, hold it away from the deck. Ask: "Do you want this card for your poker hand or for mine?" If the spectator wants the card, drop it on the table. If he rejects it, shove it into the body of the deck about halfway down in the deck with a good two-thirds of the card projecting from the deck as in Fig. 43, #1. ·

Do this again and again until the spectator has chosen 5 cards and, by rejection, has in effect chosen the 5 cards for your poker hand. Seemingly the spectator has controlled everything. All 10 choices have been free as the wind.

Five cards are face-down on the table, 5 cards are face-down in the middle of the deck, slightly fanned as in #1. To the audience the effect is that you strip out the 5 cards from the deck as in #2 with your left hand while holding the deck in your right hand.

Drop the deck from your right hand on top of the 5 cards in your left hand and square up the deck. Say: "You chose five cards for yourself, let's see what you have." The spectator turns over his hand and has a good poker hand, which may be anything from 4 of a kind to a full house or 3 of a kind. Whatever he gets, you turn the deck over, revealing the 5 bottom cards on the deck, and show that you have done a little better than he has. You have a royal flush!

There is a set-up but it is delightfully simple. On the bottom of the deck, place a royal flush.

On top of the deck place 2 fours of a kind, let's say eights and nines, and a pair of jacks. Arrange the eights and nines alternately, ending up with the jacks—8-9-8-9-8-9-8-9-J-J.

You're practically ready, for the shuffles present no problem since you just hold back the top 10 or 11 cards and the bottom 5. It's almost not fair to call this a false-shuffle. Finish up with any decent false-cut (see page 178). The effect is so strong that if this false-shuffle and false-cut business bothers you, you can dispense with it.

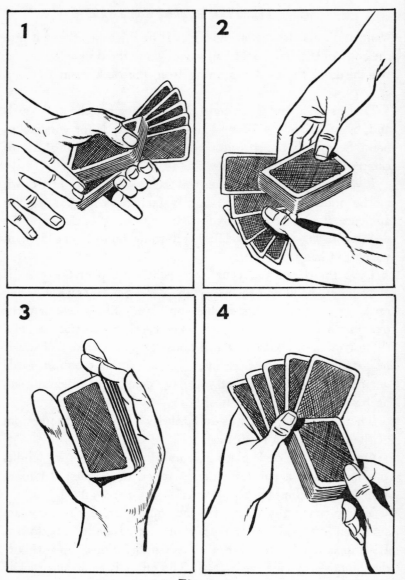

Fig. 43

Hold the deck in the left hand in the dealing position. Push off the top card and ask the spectator if he wants the card or wants you to have it. If he wants it, drop it on the table. If he doesn't, push it halfway into the deck in the middle of the deck.

Proceed as in the effect until he has 5 cards and you have 5 cards sticking fan-wise out of the deck. Now comes the delightful move; it is so deceptive you can fool yourself with it.

This is a gentle, effortless kind of move. Fig. 43, #1, shows the deck held at the finger tips of the right hand. The base of the deck and the left thumb and palm support part of the weight of the deck.

The tip of the right middle finger makes a break in the side of the deck. Be sure the break is above the block of 5 cards on the bottom of the deck, and below the fan of cards in the middle of the deck. Don't worry about counting to just above the bottom stock of 5.

As soon as you have made the break with the finger tip, transfer the break to the tip of the middle finger and bring the lion's share of the deck up a little, enough to free the block of cards which now lies quiescent in the palm, and encircled by the caged fingers of the left hand. Move the left hand with its block of cards (hidden by the fanned cards in the deck) upward to the top of the deck. The rest of the deck is held statue-still by the thumb and middle finger of the right hand. This action is shown in #2. The left thumb should be on top of the deck and fan.

When the left hand has come all the way up as far as it can without revealing the block of cards lying on its palm (see #3 which has been drawn without the right hand) the left thumb comes down gently on top of the fan as shown (#4) and pulls it free of the deck (also and incidentally, the fan and the cards below all drop onto the hidden block in the left hand).

Now the left hand freezes and the right hand holding the remainder of the deck comes back toward the body and drops the deck onto the cards in the left hand.

The effect to the audience is that you merely have pulled the fanned 5 cards out of the deck and put them on the bottom of the deck. This is the best switch of a group of cards that you're ever going to find in print, so please study it well, and use it sparingly.

The title? It simply means Bruce and Dai Vernon.

DALEY'S DELIGHT

"Follow the Leader" is one of the most delightful card effects I know. It is efficient in that a small amount of preparation accomplishes a great effect, and in that a minimum of skill is needed.

In Dr. Daley's method there are no sleights and the whole effect is accomplished through the aid of only one extra card of each color. Run through the effect with a packet of cards and I think you will find you have added a fine card trick to your repertoire.

Run through any deck and take out 10 red and 10 black cards. While culling or running through the deck, add a black to the rear of the red packet and a red to the rear of the black. In its simple, non-sleight handling, the effect then proceeds as follows.

Talk about the children's game of Follow the Leader and explain that there is a way of playing the game with the red and black cards in a deck.

Drop your two packets of reds and blacks on the table. Pick up the reds, face up in your left hand (which, you remember, has a black card at the back of the packet), and count off 9 red cards, showing each one clearly. On the count of 10 leave the tenth red card with the black one hidden behind it in your left hand. Drop the 9 counted cards back on top of these and drop the whole batch face up on the table.

Repeat with the other packet. Unlike other methods of doing this trick, the audience has now seen 10 cards of each color.

Once you have counted the cards aloud never refer to the number of cards involved again. At the end of the effect you will have used 11 cards instead of 10, but no one ever spots this discrepancy because of the handling.

You now have two packets of cards on the table in front of you. Pick a red card from the red heap and a black card from the black heap. Explain that these are the leader cards. Place them at right angles to the packets, face up on the table.

Deal off, still face up, 3 cards from each packet as you explain how children play Follow the Leader. Show that reds go on reds and blacks on black.

No tricks so far. You then turn the packets of cards face down and move the leader cards, with the dealt-off cards on them, from right to left and left to right. Despite this switch you show, as you deal off and turn them face up, a matching black card on the black packet and a matching red on the red packet. The cards have followed the leader! (First change.)

Move the leader cards again from right to left and vice versa. Again deal off and show that the cards have literally followed the leader. (Second change.)

Next comes a brazen bit of business. Deal off from the face down packets one card from the packet to the leader position from each heap. Naturally, they match, but don't comment or show this yet. Instead, move the leader heaps from right to left and left to right with these cards in place.

Turn up these face-down cards and they match. (Third change.) Say, "Of course, if you reverse the heaps rather than the leaders, the same magical thing happens." Turn over the top cards on each of the heaps. They match. (Fourth change.)

For a completely sleightless method you finish by dealing off the remaining cards and showing they match. You have managed four complete seeming reversals of position by the aid of one stranger card in each packet.

For the sleight of hand devotee, deal off 3 cards at this time on each leader packet. This leaves 2 face-down cards on the table. Pick these up on top of each other, cater-cornered, and show their position. In turning face down, reverse their positions and deal off. The cards match again.

The late Dr. Daley's delight at this point, however, was a sleight that is not a sleight. Pick the red card face-up in the right hand between the thumb and forefinger, palm up. Pick up the black card between fore and middle fingers at the extreme tips of the fingers (Fig. 44, #1). Hand is palm up. Place backs of hands on table and show positions of colors. The red packet on the table is to the right, the black to the left.

The cards in your hands are shown and turned face down. Now bring the right hand toward the left and place the black card in your right hand between the thumb and forefinger of the left (#2), simultaneously putting the red card from your left hand between the fore and middle finger tips of the right hand.

If you continued as is normal the cards would reverse their positions, but you don't. As the hands meet and the cards are exchanged, your normal tendency will be to bring your left hand back to the left, and your right to the right. Don't do this. Instead, continue with your right hand going to the left, and with your left hand going to the right (#3). This has a curious feeling and you will have to force your hands to do it. Drop the cards from your hands as your right hand comes far to the left and your left far to the right.

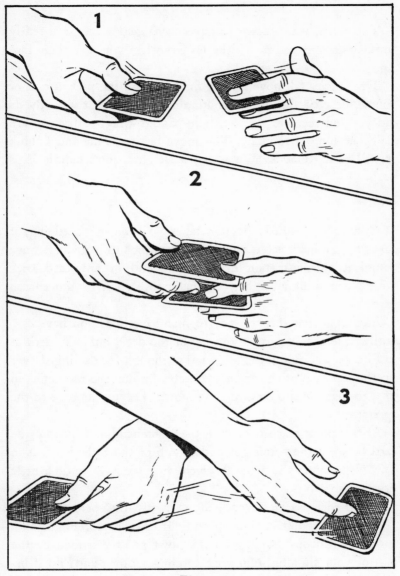

Fig. 44

The cards, which seem to have exchanged places, are really unreversed and will match the leaders when you turn them face up.

This suggested move for the final cards in the packet, can, of course, be used during the routine of follow the leader. By its aid you can seem to switch whole packets when really you are doing nothing of the kind. This move fascinates me and I think it will you. Remember, it is not a sleight; don't handle it as such.

A. P.

Although this little flourish takes no time in the doing, it takes an unconscionable number of drawings to explain. I have found it aids a certain fillip to the end of any card trick where you want a slightly dramatic revelation of the chosen card.

Assuming that through any of many methods you have controlled the chosen card to the top of the deck, hold the deck as in Fig. 45, #1, flat in the left hand as though for dealing. Lever up the top card as shown in #2, and continue the motion as in #3, so that the chosen card hinges over, keeping its back to the spectators.

At this point reach over with the right hand and pick up the card between the forefinger and thumb of the right hand as in #4. Next comes the point at which you may have to do a little practicing.

The card looks from the front as in #5, the spectator's side. Next, allow the card to drop away from your forefinger and, as the card drops, hinging on the pivot point provided by the ball of your thumb, bring your forefinger down and clip it between the tip of the forefinger and thumb. The spectator's view of this is shown in #6.

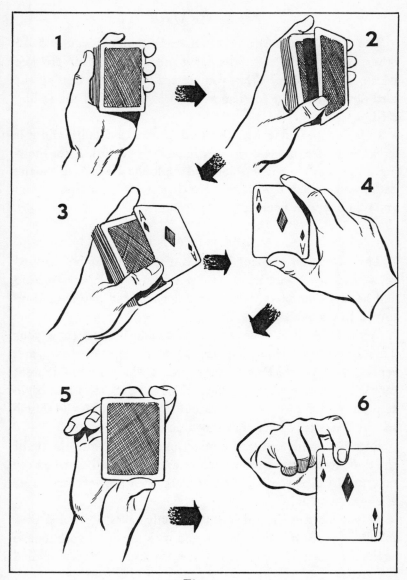

Fig. 45

The action is unhurried because A. P. comes to your aid. In other words, as the card falls flat it presses against *air pressure* which slows it down. What you are really doing is chasing the card down with your forefinger which is just behind the falling card.

I use this maneuver with two cards after a double lift and it is a real convincer that you are only handling one card. After showing a "double" in this fashion and replacing both cards on the deck, your audience will be more than a little surprised when you continue with your double lift routine.

BRRRRTTTT!

This is just an incident in the course of any ambitious card routine in which you may indulge your fancy. It is surprising and has a sound effect; whatever other merit it may have is up to you to discover.

With the deck in your left hand, double lift and show your ambitious card which, in Fig. 46, #3, is the eight of spades, and replace on the deck. Pick off the top card which is an indifferent card and, as you push it into the back of the deck as in #1, begin to push the top card of the deck out of position with the thumb so that it is cater-cornered as shown in #1.

Push the indifferent card further into the deck with the tip of the right forefinger as shown and as you do so, pull down on the outermost tip of the top card on deck with the left forefinger as shown in #2.

As you do this (the whole thing only takes a fraction of a minute in performing) make a sound with the tip of your tongue against the back of your teeth which produces the noise spelled "brrrrtttt."

The sound should be simultaneous with the left forefinger levering the top card on the deck over and outward. It is held

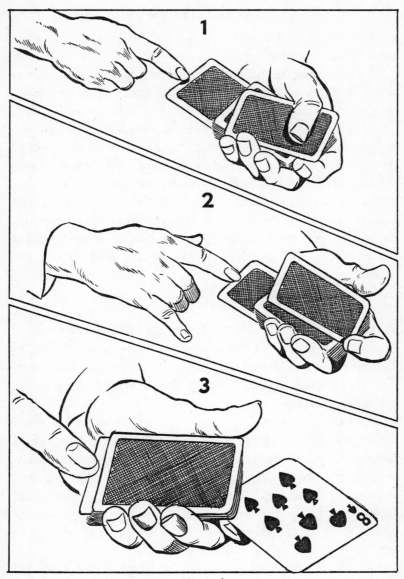

Fig. 46

as shown in #3 for a second and then you go back into your orthodox card routine.

The effect is an odd one and I have found that for some reason people find it funny; and certainly a card trick that makes people giggle has a place in your repertoire.

When I use this move I find there is enough surprise inherent in it so that I can take the face-up card away from the deck in the right hand and flip it in the air, as at the same time, dropping the left hand with the deck to my side and using my body as a rest, I reverse the top card on the deck. Catching the spun card I drop it on top of the reversed card on the deck face-up, and a double lift gets me back into position with an added card for the ambitious card and I am ready for the next step in the routine.

FILLIP

Heaven knows there are too few sleight of hand ways of revealing a chosen card. This is one of my own, and I like it. There's not much more to say about it. It's strictly for finger-flingers, although it's easy. It's not for the school that feels art lies in concealing art.

Bring the chosen card to the bottom of the deck. Hold the deck in the right hand as in Fig. 47, #2. Allow the bottom card to drop down, pivoting it on the middle two fingers. Just allow it to drop down as shown, being sure that the angle prevents anyone from seeing it. Next, with the left hand which is not shown in #1, take the top card off the deck as though you expected it to be the chosen card. You are put out when it is not.

Let this card drop onto your palm the long way and seemingly place it on the bottom of the deck. Really replace it on the bottom of the deck under the downward card as in #2. The re-

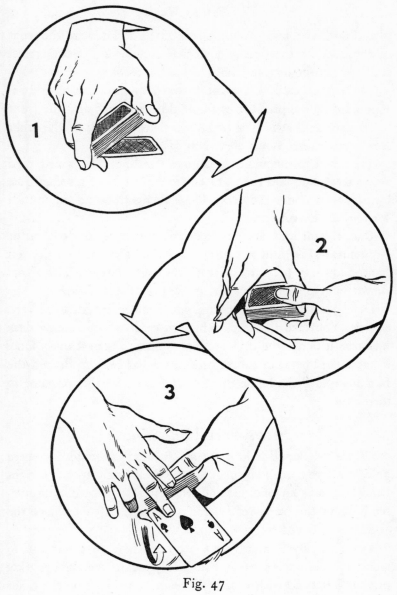

Fig. 47

placed card is brought from the rear of the deck toward the front of the deck, as the side of your left forefinger presses against the inside of the bottom card.

The chosen card will pivot forward as shown in #3. It is supported by the pressure of the middle finger against the front of the card as shown. The pressure against the side of the other forefinger is also shown clearly in #3.

The effect to the audience is quite startling. The wrong card seems to change into the right one in a fraction of a second just by passing it under the deck. There seems to be no time at all for any chicanery.

Once the card has appeared you will find that the deck, in the right fingers, is right over the left palm. Drop it into the left hand and carry the card off with the right fingers. This is not shown but you will find that it happens automatically.

Done with the deck face-up, you have a fine delayed card change. You take the face-up bottom card off the face-up deck and pass it under the deck seemingly just to turn it over. Once it has turned over, of course, the switch has been made and the face-down card can be dropped on the table for the spectator to turn over.

SIMON-EASE [*Bill Simon*]

Shuffle a deck and hold it in the left hand as though you were going to have a peek taken. Riffle the deck freely with the right hand and have anyone tell you when to stop. There is no nonsense about this; you really, for a change, do stop where the spectator tells you to.

You cut off—seemingly at the point where they tell you to stop—and place this cut to one side. Idly cut the remaining packet in your left hand with your right hand. Then pick up the other packet and place it back on top of the one in your left hand.

Despite all this freedom you now have the selected card on the bottom of the deck.

It will help if you hold a deck in your left hand and proceed with the directions. Riffle with right hand and stop anywhere, as in Fig. 48, #1. Cut off this packet and display the card on the face of it. When you bring this packet back to the left hand jog it down about a quarter of an inch.

Release your right hand, hold for a second to gesture with it. Immediately bring the right hand back to the packet and cut off above the jog at the inner side of the deck. Don't try to cut off only one card, just cut above it as shown in #2.

Cut off this packet and place to one side. Gesture at it, and while you speak, idly cut the packet in your left hand with your right. This cuts the chosen card to the bottom of this packet. Now you can replace the right hand packet on top of the left hand one and shuffle, keeping the chosen card on the bottom all the time.

The move takes a fraction of a second to make and is completely covered. There is nothing for the most suspicious eye to catch.

Instead of breaking the move in the middle as above, you can do it all at one time. Riffle the deck, stop, have the card looked at, jog the top packet down, cut off above the chosen card and proceed as above, without placing the top packet on the table. You just cut it to the bottom of the deck and then cut to the chosen card.

TWO BLADES [*Bill Simon*]

In this revelation, a knife is found above and below a selected card so that the card is sandwiched between blades of steel. It makes an odd looking and startling denouement.

The method is simple, clean, and it works. Have a paper napkin and two knives handy. Table knives will do, although the

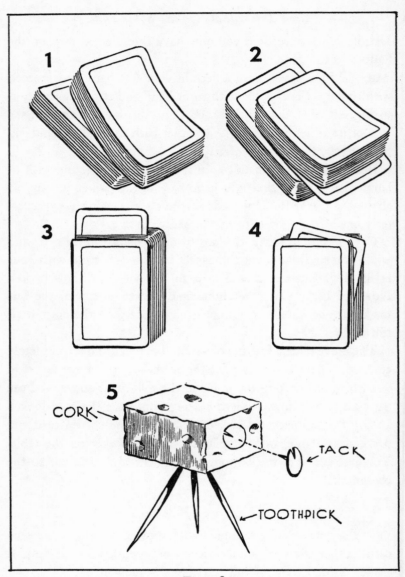

1

2

3

4

5

CORK →

→ TACK

← TOOTHPICK

Fig. 48

odder looking the knives the more spectacular the stunt will look. Use any deck and after it has been shuffled, any card is taken. It is put back into the deck but before it is shoved all the way into the deck, pause and show it as in Fig. 48, #3, so the spectators can have one last look at it.

The only "work" is done a second later. As you shove the, card all the way into the deck, bring it to the right as shown in #4. With the card projecting this way you can place your right hand over it in such a way that you can grasp the deck and hide the projecting edges and tap the far side of the deck on the table.

Having tapped the left hand edge of the deck, pick up the paper napkin and as soon as the deck is wrapped tightly you can relax. All that remains to be done is to pick up the first knife and jab it into the far, narrow edge of the deck coming up from below. The tip of the knife will be stopped by the projecting lip of the card. You have to be a bit careful of this for the jog is small.

The other knife you bring down on the side of the deck and you can be more cavalier about your handling in this case, for here your jog is bigger and more easily felt.

With the knives stuck into the deck, place the deck on the table, dilate on the impossibility of what you are attempting, and then rip the paper off the top of the deck. Allow one of the spectators to lift the packet above the top of knife. Before them is a card between two blades.

You will find that, using the same motion you would with chop sticks, you can pick the card up using the knives as the chop sticks. You then have the chosen card practically untouched by human hands.

MINICAM [*Bill Simon*]

You will need the "camera" described later, a deck of cards, a tiny card a half-inch by a quarter-inch in size, a piece of blank paper to match, a pencil, and a card on the bottom of the deck to match the miniature card.

The blank piece of paper is on the table. The miniature card is on top of the second card from the top of the deck. That is, it is concealed by the top card on the deck. You can now force the bottom card on the deck, or just take it off the deck, turn it over face-up and say casually, "Here, we'll use this card to see if this sensitized paper I bought in a photographic store will do a trick for me."

Show the bottom card, the king of spades, for example, and lay it on the table. Pick up the little blank paper and lay it on the center of the top card on the deck. Place the force card, the king, on top of this for a moment, getting ready for a double lift, and "remember" that you forgot to have the paper initialed. Pick off the top two cards as one and have the spectator X or initial the paper. This is really the photo card. Drop it face-down on the table. Place the double lifted cards back on top of the photo card.

Deal off the top card onto the table. As you do this, keep your thumb across the top of the deck so that when the card comes off, your thumb covers the blank bit of paper there. You'll have no trouble with this if you tilt the deck up and away from the spectators. Press your thumb down, covering the bit of paper, and drop the king on top of the small card on the table.

Patter, and then lift the little card on the table with the right fingers. Don't show the card side of paper. Bluff and say, "Hmmm nothing has happened yet. Ah, I forgot the camera."

Your left thumb and forefinger gripping the little bit of paper go to your pocket for the camera. Drop the paper there and come out with the "camera." This is simply made as shown in Fig. 48, #5. You need a little block of balsa wood, painted black, three toothpicks jammed in the bottom of the balsa block to make a tripod, and a thumb tack shoved in the front of the block for the lens.

Show this and place it on the table. Pick up the initialed little card, concealing the face of it, and hold it to the back of the camera. Hold the big card in front of the lens. Count to three and turn the little card over. There the audience sees a tiny replica of the big card.

You see why you don't have to worry about forcing the card. So much happens that by the time the revelation is made the spectators are not worrying about the card that was chosen, but *how* the little card was printed on the tiny, initialed, previously shown blank card.

The handling of the whole thing is easy, the prop is cute and the effect is strong.

TABLED [*Bill Simon*]

There are many methods for seeming to slam a card clear through a table top. The handling in this particular method is simple in the extreme.

Get a deck of cards and follow directions. Have a card selected (use the control in "Simon-Ease") and bring it to the bottom of the deck.

Shuffle a few times, keeping the selected card on the bottom. This should not trouble the most fumble-fingered. As you shuffle the last time, bring the deck near the edge of the table getting a break above the chosen card with the right hand.

With the left hand cut off the top half of the deck and place it away from you toward the center of the table. As you do this, the right hand brings its packet to the edge of the table and drops the card into your lap. This is completely covered by the large action of the left hand bringing its packet forward. Once the card has been dropped into the lap, the right hand brings its packet forward to the center of the table and completes the cut.

The action looks normal, as though you had just cut the deck.

With the deck in the center of the table, patter about your ability to smash the deck and force the chosen card to the bottom of the deck. Whack the deck with your palm and then pick up the deck and look at the bottom card hopefully. It isn't the chosen card. You are distrait. Suddenly "remember" that perhaps you used too much force. At this moment your hand is under the table and has picked the chosen card off your lap.

As you say, "Perhaps I slammed the deck too hard . . ." snap the card under the table and then bring it into view. A quickie admittedly, but a clean one.

AGAIN [*Bill Simon*]

Many years ago the late Ted Annemann created an effect called "Insto-Transpo," using a double-backed card. Annemann later devised a method by which it could be done without the gimmicked card. The main drawback to both of Annemann's methods was that the handling was not open; a bluff call of the name of a card being necessary. Since the spectators could not be shown the face of the card it left doubts in an excellent effect.

Here is a method which is simpler, more direct, and more convincing than any other I know.

In effect, a spectator freely selects a card and places his initials on the face of it. This card is placed in the spectator's pocket. Performer does the same thing. A change is commanded to take place. Spectator reaches into his pocket and finds the performer's card, while the spectator's card is found in the magician's pocket!

An amazing change. The initials, of course, check properly, further to baffle the spectators.

An extra card from a deck that has the same back and color of the deck you will use, is required. Most magicians have a pet brand of cards (Fox Lake, for example) so it is a simple matter to acquire an extra card. For descriptive purposes assume the card is the two of hearts.

Place your initials on the face of the upper, left-hand corner of this card. Use pencil and write lightly so that it is easily erased when the effect is concluded. Place this extra card in the deck. Go through any card tricks you desire with this extra card in the deck, for the odds are 52 to 1 that it will not be seen by the spectators. Also, if it *is* seen, there is slim chance of anyone noticing your initials if written lightly on the card, as suggested.

You now have an extra card in the deck with your initials in the upper, left-hand corner.

When ready to do the trick, run through the cards, faces towards you, and under the pretense of removing the joker place the initialed two of hearts on the *bottom* of the deck and the regular two of hearts on *top* of the deck. You can do this set-up during the course of a preceding trick. Shuffle the cards, not disturbing the top or bottom cards, and have the spectator freely choose a card from the center of the deck. Take the card and place it face-up on the bottom of the deck, displaying it for all to see. Hand the spectator the deck and a pencil and tell him to place his initials on the card he selected, using the deck as a support to aid in his initialing the card.

Spectator initials his card and returns the deck to you. Tell the spectator to open his coat pocket as you are going to place his card in his pocket. Double-lift the spectator's card from the bottom of the deck with your right hand. Turn deck face-down with your left hand. Place the card(s) face-up on the face-down deck. Review what has transpired and then turn the two cards face-down on the deck, dealing the top one into your right hand. Place, or have this card placed, into the spectator's waiting pocket.

Apparently you have had the spectator select a card, initial it and place it in his pocket. Actually, his initialed card is on top of the deck. Under it is an unmarked two of hearts, the duplicate of which is now in spectator's pocket with your initials on it. Give the deck a false cut and/or false shuffle.

Say, "I'll use this card." Double-lift the two top cards and place them face-up on top of the deck. Initial it in the identical spot that the duplicate (now in spectator's pocket) was initialed. Show the card to everyone. Turn the two top cards over as one, deal into your right hand, and place them in your right pocket.

Review what has happened and start to build up the effect. As you patter, place the deck in your left pocket. When it is in the pocket, slip off the top card (two of hearts) and casually withdraw the deck, minus this card. Place the deck on the table. This is done during the patter, with your right side facing the audience. Dramatically snap your fingers and command the cards to change places. Have spectator withdraw the card from his pocket. It is found to be your card. Have spectator reach into your right pocket (which should be empty except for the card) and withdraw the card. It is found to be his card! Show the cards and call attention to the fact that they are still initialed. To all appearances you have accomplished a miracle!

DOUBLE-LIFT DECEPTIONS [*Clayton Rawson*]

Variations of a single theme, these four tricks produce diverse effects through the use of the same basic sleight—the Double Lift. Here is the manipulation on which all four tricks depend.

Hold the deck in the dealing position and riffle the outer left corner with the thumb, asking a spectator to stop you at any time. When he does, lift off the cards above the break and hand them to him. Release one more card with the thumb, tap its back with the right forefinger and say, "I want you to note and remember this card."

The right hand moves forward to pick up the card by the outer left corner and, just as the fingers of the right hand cover the outer edges of the deck (Fig. 49, #1), the thumb releases a second card. The right thumb and forefinger grip both cards, (at point shown) you display them as one, and then replace them on the deck, the left thumb immediately pushing the top card slightly to the right. Tell the spectator, "Now you cut the cards you hold into two portions and we'll place your card between them like meat in a sandwich." Take off your top card, insert it among his and tell him to shuffle thoroughly. If properly done, the spectator now thinks his card is among those he is shuffling when actually you have it on top of the half deck you hold. Almost anything should be possible from this point on. Here are a few variations.

1. *Right in front of your nose:* Undercut about half the cards you hold and place them on top of the deck. Hold a break with the tip of the little finger between the two packets of cards. Fan the cards and apparently take out one card at random, actually forcing the chosen card on yourself. Hand the remainder of the deck to the spectator and tell him to shuffle them in with the others just to make it harder.

Then announce that while the spectator is shuffling you will write a prediction on the face of the card you hold—a prediction which will tell *the exact position of the chosen card after the shuffle has been completed!* On the face of the chosen card write the words: *It's right here!* and put the card to one side.

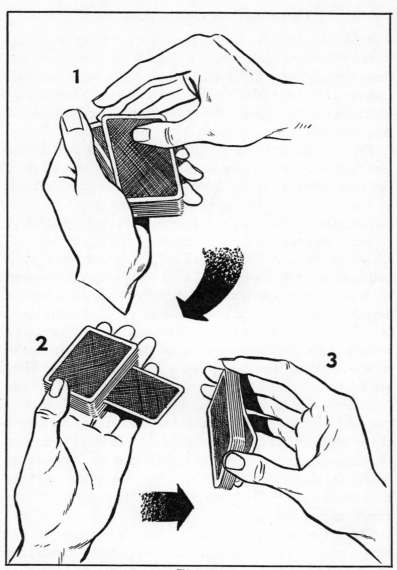

Fig. 49

Drive home the fact that the spectator is himself shuffling the cards and the fact that you will not touch them again. "In spite of this," you announce, "I have already predicted the location the chosen card will occupy *after* the shuffle!" When the spectator says he is satisfied no one could now possibly know the location of the chosen card tell him that as an extra added attraction for this one performance only, you will also name the card that he is thinking of—and do so!

After he admits you are correct, ask some other person to pick up the prediction card and read aloud your prediction of the present location of the chosen card. He reads, "It's right here!" and shows that he holds it in his right hand!

2. *Magic taught in one easy lesson:* Have a card chosen in the same manner as before and, giving the spectator what he thinks is his card and asking him to shuffle it in with his other cards, turn to another person. "Mr. Jones," you say, "I'm now going to ask you to do a trick for us. Have you ever performed as a magician before? No? Well, that makes it harder, but perhaps you'll have beginner's luck. Do you know the name of the card this gentleman (indicate first spectator) is thinking of? And do you know exactly where his card is in the shuffled deck? You don't? Do you think you could find it? You're not sure? Hmmm, that's bad. The first thing you need to learn is that a magician must always have complete self-confidence."

Turn to the first spectator. "Will you give 'The Great Jones' the cards you have, please. Now, professor, I want you to concentrate and read Mr. Smith's mind—then run through the cards and pick out the one he is thinking of." Wait for him to do it and when he admits he's having difficulty, say, "Oh, come now. It's not that difficult. Besides, you're trying to do it the hard way. Look, this is much easier. We'll take any other card at random." Double-lift and turn up the 2 cards on top of the half deck you hold. "This six of clubs, for instance." Turn both cards face down again and deal off the top one.

Hold your half deck in the left hand, fingers at outer end, thumb at inner end as though you were going to give the cards an overhand shuffle with the left hand. "Hold the cards like this." Pick up the dealt-off card, push it into the side of the deck you hold, about an inch (#2), and tell Jones, "I want you to take this six of clubs and insert it anywhere into the cards you hold in this manner." Then remove and give him the card (which is, of course, actually the chosen card) and have him repeat your action.

"Now push the card quickly so that it goes right through the deck and comes out on the other side. That's fine, Mr. Smith, will you please tell us the name of the card on which you have been concentrating? The queen of spades? Mr. Jones, take the six of clubs out of the deck you hold—show it to the audience, and take a bow." He does so and finds that the six has mysteriously been transformed into the chosen queen of spades.

Shake his hand. Congratulate him and add, "I am sure you'll have a lot of fun doing that trick for your friends."

3. *Stream-Lined Hypnotism:* This variation requires the use of one duplicate card which is placed on the bottom of the deck. The card that matches it is on top. Have a spectator stop your riffle in the usual manner and lift off all the cards above the break, being careful to let everyone see that you cut exactly where he has indicated. Give him the upper portion of the deck, double-lift the next two cards, show it to the spectator, replace on the deck immediately, then deal off the top one and have him shuffle it among those he holds in the usual manner.

Hold the remainder of the cards in position to begin an overhand shuffle; thumb-count two cards at the face of the deck, and hold a break there with the right thumb (#3). Shuffle and drop the last two cards together on top of deck. Cut the deck and hold a break with the left little finger. Ask a second spectator to stop you as you riffle the cards. Reach out with the right hand to cut the cards at the break held by the thumb but let the right fingers cover the outer end of the deck just as the cut is made. You appear to cut at the point where the spectator stopped you, but instead you actually lift off all the cards above the break at the rear by the little finger. (As far as is known, this force was a Ted Annemann secret and has not previously appeared in print. It will be referred to hereafter as the *Riffle-Force*.)

Give the spectator the cut-off cards, double-lift the next two and show them. (The spectator will be looking at the duplicate card that was originally on the bottom of the deck.) Replace the cards, deal off the top one, put it in his deck and have him shuffle.

At any time between now and the conclusion of the trick, palm off the duplicate card now on top of the deck and get rid of it in your pocket. The card noted by the first spectator is now with the cards the second spectator holds and vice versa. You can, of course, simply command the two chosen cards to change places. Or you can use a little fancier and more unusual finish as follows.

"Modern hypnotism," you say, "has been developed to the point where it is extremely dangerous. A good hypnotist can hypnotize anyone almost instantly and without the subject being aware of it. I'll demonstrate." Turn to the first spectator, ask him to look into your eyes, concentrate briefly, then snap your fingers. "He is now in a trance and doesn't know it." Do the same to the second person, but pretend that he is a bit harder to hypnotize. "You apparently have more will power." Snap your fingers twice. "But you are now in an even deeper trance than your friend here. Remind me to bring you out of it later. If I don't the consequences may be serious."

Turn back to the first person. "These two persons do not appear to be hypnotized and neither of them believe that they are. But watch!" Turn to the first person and say, "Look at my eyes. When I snap my fingers your memory of the card you chose will be completely destroyed. You will forget it utterly." Snap fingers. "And I shall now project into your mind in place of the missing memory, the name of a new card, one that you couldn't possibly have chosen!" Snap fingers.

Turn quickly to the second person and command, "Think of your card! Your mental image is fading . . . fading . . . and is [snap fingers] gone! Another image forms in your mind, the image of a card my mind is projecting into yours, the image of a card you have not and could not have seen!" (Snap fingers.)

Turn back to the first person. "You think you still remember the name of the card you chose, don't you? All right, just run through the cards you have and pick it out, and you . . . [turn to second person] do the same." Neither of them will be able to find their cards.

Tell the first spectator, "You see? Your card is still there, but you don't recognize it because you are now thinking of another card . . . the card this gentleman [point to second spectator] chose and has among his cards. I'll prove it. Name your card." When he names it have the second person run through his cards and take out the card named!

Turn to the second spectator. "I told you I would erase the memory of the card you chose and replace it with the mental image of a card you could not possibly have seen. I call your attention to the fact that you could not have seen any of the cards this gentleman [the first spectator] holds because he had them *before* you chose your card. Please name the card you think you saw."

He names it and the first spectator finds it among his cards. Look at each person, snap your fingers and bring them out of the trance, or follow this effect with some other pseudo-hypnotic effect.

4. *The absent-minded spectator:* This is a variation of the foregoing effect, in which the first spectator actually does forget, cannot name the card he saw, and names as his card the first spectator chose, that has been in full view in the first spectator's breast pocket all the time.

The deck has the following three cards on top in this order, reading from the top down; a duplicate card, a card with a blank face, an indifferent card, the card, the card that matches the duplicate.

Cut the deck and hold a break. Use the Riffle-Force described in the second paragraph under "Stream-Lined Hypnotism." Double-lift the two top cards. Tell the spectator to try to keep a poker face and not let his facial muscles betray the name of the card to you. Warn him that when he looks at the card he must not say a word but must concentrate on the card he sees as intently as possible. Show him the blank card without letting anyone else see it. Then place the card(s) back toward the audience in his breast pocket. Shove them all the way in, leave the blank down in the pocket. Pull the outer card up and leave it projecting. Warn the spectator not to touch it at any time.

Replace the cut-off cards on the deck and hold a break between the two portions. Use the Riffle-Force on second spectator. Give him cards above the break and double-lift, showing him the duplicate of the card in the first spectator's pocket. Replace the deck, deal off the top card, and have him shuffle it in among those he holds.

Then, at your convenience, palm off the top card (the duplicate) and dispose of it in your pocket. The rest is build-up and presentation. Tell the first spectator you will make him forget the name of the card he saw and make his mental image of that card a complete blank. Ask him to name it. He fails.

Turn to the second person and tell him you will not only make him forget the name of the card he chose but will go further and replace the memory with the name of a card he has not seen at all. Give him the hypnotic business as in the foregoing effect and ask him to name the card he thinks he chose. "Impossible!" you say. "That is the name of the card the first person chose and forgot and which has been in full view since *before* you chose your card—in his breast pocket!" The spectator removes the card and the situation is found to be exactly as you have stated. (Curtain.)

This warning shouldn't be necessary but some magicians do peculiar things. These tricks all depend upon the same basic moves, so don't do more than one of them at any one performance. Both the double-lift and the Riffle-Force are extremely useful and undetectable sleights if done well and *used sparingly*.

BIDDLED [*Bill Simon*]

Here is as saucy a use for the Biddle move as I have ever seen. I'm happy Bill Simon thought of it for two reasons. It gives me a chance to explain the move I think is one of the most valuable weapons a card handler can have in his armory of sleights and it serves as a clean method for a startling effect.

Before getting down to the mechanics of the method, however, Bill's effect is that he shows a series of cards—ten or twelve—and then sets them so they are face-up and face-down alternately. He counts them one by one, thus proving that every other card is face-up and face-down.

That done, he spreads the cards and "hey, presto," the cards have righted themselves!

Or, a series of cards can be shown to be alternately red and black, and at the finish they are shown to have been divided into all blacks and all reds.

You can see the possibilities!

To work: Take 10 cards and set them face up and face down alternately. Holding them in left hand as in Fig. 50, #1, between the finger tips at the far end and the ball of thumb at the near end push the right hand towards them with the thumb on top side of the top card. Pull this card off to the right. In the drawings in Fig. 50 this first card is face up, and is numbered 1.

Allow this card to drop on the palm of the right hand and place left hand packet over this card as shown in #2. Again pull off the top card (number 2) into the right hand with the thumb. Allow it to jog itself to the left along the length of the card as shown in #3.

Card 2 is face down and is the one you are going to steal. You are going to steal it from the right hand back onto the bottom of the packet of cards in the left hand.

This action is shown in #3 and #4. As you place the packet of cards over cards 1 and 2, preparatory to pulling card number 3 off the top of the packet, you will find that the tips of the middle and third fingers press upwards on it. All you need do is add it to the bottom of the left hand packet, retaining it by the tips of thumb and middle fingers.

Card number 3, when it has been drawn off by the right thumb, covers the action of card 2 being stolen.

Once this basic series has been learned the action becomes automatic. If you have followed the description and if you continue to pull off and steal alternate cards, you will find after

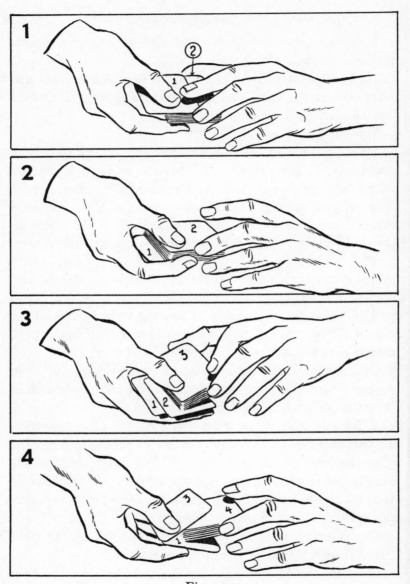

Fig. 50

showing the 10 cards seemingly alternated that you have really divided them into 5 face-up and 5 face-down cards.

If you do a half-pass at this point the cards will, of course, be in their normal order, with all backs one way and all faces the other.

By experimenting with this use of the Biddle move you'll find you can have a card selected from the packet and, at the finish, show it is the only card that has not reversed itself while all the others have righted themselves. Or you can separate reds from blacks ad infinitum.

THE CARD IN THE WALLET

The "purest" method of performing the classical effect, where a chosen card appears in your wallet, demands a slight amount of skill.

As in all methods you begin by having a card freely selected, initialed by the spectator, and returned to the deck. Using the system of card control described on page 122, or by the use of the Hindu Shuffle or the classic pass, bring the chosen card to the bottom of the deck.

At this point challenge the audience, claiming, "Here is a trick that never fails! I defy you to catch me on this one!" Irritated at your arrogance, your audience will be on its mental toes. At this point ask the person who selected the card to think of a number between 1 and 10. While all attention is on the spectator perform the steal shown in Fig. 51. The chosen card is the bottom one on the deck. Holding the deck in your right hand between the thumb at the near end and the middle, ring and pinky finger of your right (see #1 and #2), press the bottom card on the deck against the palm of the left and peel it off the bottom of the deck in the action of bringing the deck from this position up to the thumb and tips of the left fingers as shown in

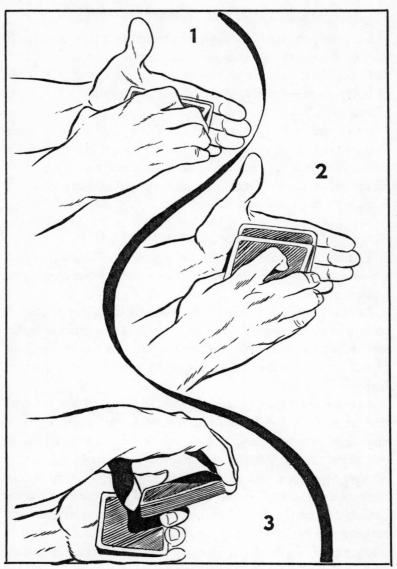

Fig. 51

#3. In performing, the effect is that you have merely adjusted the deck as you transfer it from the right hand to the left. The selected card is now palmed in the left hand, and concealed by the deck at the finger tips.

Ask the spectator to concentrate on the number he has decided on mentally.

Prior to the performance of this effect you have folded your wallet backwards on itself as shown in Fig. 52, #1, and placed the folded wallet into the inner breast pocket of your jacket as shown.

Drop the deck from your left hand onto the table-top in front of the spectator who is thinking of a number.

As you drop the deck, instantly bring your left hand (with the palmed card) from the table, under the jacket lapel toward your breast pocket. To facilitate this, use your right hand as shown in Fig. 52, #3, to pull the right hand lapel outward from your body. Your left hand pushes the palmed card into the opening in your wallet, so that the card is under the celluloid window that generally reveals your auto license, or identification. This whole sequence is done in one fast movement while you say, "I'm so sure this trick never fails that . . ." When you say this, lift your wallet out of your pocket and allow it to turn on itself so that the wallet is no longer turned back on itself but is in its normal position. This means that the chosen card is now safely hidden under the celluloid window.

Take the wallet from your pocket and slap it down on the table on top of the deck of cards as you say, "I'm going to bet the contents of my wallet the trick will work!"

Push the wallet off the deck onto the table and ask the spectator what number he thought of.

Assuming he says, "Five," count off four cards, pick up the fifth card back-up, and snap it with your fingers as you say, "It

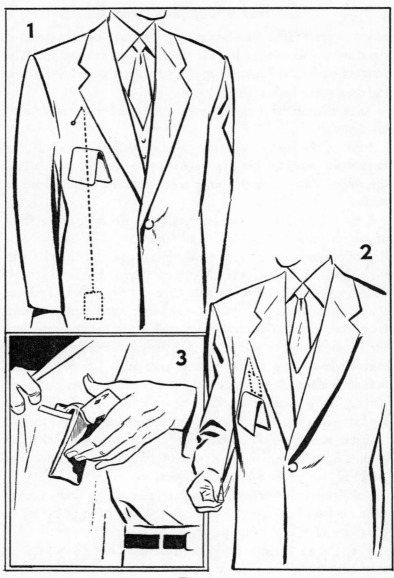

Fig. 52

would be quite a trick if I had made your selected, initialed card appear at the thought-of number down from the top of the deck, wouldn't it?"

The audience will agree that it would be quite a feat.

Turn the card over and show that you have failed. It is not the selected card.

Smile in the face of your failure as you say, "Well—I bet the contents of my wallet that I could find your card . . ." Push the wallet towards the spectator who selected and initialed the card.

Let him open the wallet, and bask in the gasp of surprise that will result when the audience sees the chosen card under the celluloid window inside a folded wallet!

SHOULDER CARD [*Franklin V. Taylor*]

Dr. Taylor's version of the perennial and astonishing card in pocket or wallet has some elements unlike anything ever seen.

A card is freely chosen, initialed, and a corner torn from it, then it is held by a spectator for identification. The card is shuffled back into the deck. The performer reaches into his inside breast pocket with his *empty* left hand and draws the chosen card from his pocket or shows it inside of a wallet.

There is no palming involved! No palming and no skill! A gimmick does all the work. Sound good? Well, it is, because the gimmick is a pin, a paper clip and a rubber band!

If you will link a couple of rubber bands together and pin one end of the elastic to your vest or shirt just above the top pocket, then run the elastic over your shoulder and down your back, you're almost set. The only other thing needed is a paper clip or an Excelsior clip at the far end of the elastic.

This clip is fastened to your right back pocket. The situation is that, from the clip, the elastic is stretched tautly over your shoulder and comes down in front where it is fastened to your vest.

Have a card selected, marked and a corner torn off. You have the corner torn off apparently as additional identification. Really it's a no-nonsense locator, for when the card has been shuffled back into the deck you put your hands behind your back and turn your back to the audience. With your back turned, for the first time you take the deck. Next you turn to face the audience and recapitulate the circumstances. While you are talking you riffle the deck, find the torn-cornered card, and remove it. Fasten the paper clip to the chosen card and release it. Your hands are still behind your back.

Face to the audience, you hand the deck to someone to hold. The elastic draws the card up your back and over your shoulder. Expatiating on the impossibility of what you are doing, ask for the name of the card, which of course you don't know.

Letting everyone get a good look at your empty left hand, reach under your coat and grab the card, releasing it from the clip and coming right out into view with it as though you had just taken it from your breast pocket.

If you're using the wallet, drop the card into the wallet and proceed as usual.

If there is any easier non-sleight of hand way of doing this effect, I don't know it. The only thing you'll have to practice is getting the clip on and off the card easily and clearly. But this is certainly a lot easier than learning a good bottom palm.

THE CARD IN WALLET—AGAIN

Long before I had the poise necessary to palm a card at all, I evolved this method of doing the card in the wallet. Needed are a length of thread run through the coat jacket at the position shown in Fig. 52, #1. The thread is just above the inside breast pocket. In the pocket is a wallet, turned on itself as usual.

The short length of thread protruding through the jacket has a big knot tied on it as shown. The part of the thread inside the jacket is long enough to come almost to the bottom hem of the jacket. This end has a blob of magician's wax on it.

Have card selected, initialed and returned to the deck. Control it to bottom of the deck and fan the deck backs up in front of you. Say, "It doesn't seem possible I could pick out the chosen card just by a glance at the back of the cards, does it?" Pick out a card from the center of the fan and throw it on the table back up. Close fan and square up deck in right hand.

All the audience's attention is on the card on the table. Allow the right hand, containing the deck, to drop to the side. Push the bottom card (the chosen one) off the deck, letting it slant out from the deck. Then bring the card up under the jacket and press the deck against the cloth of the jacket and so against the blob of wax under the cloth. Make sure the wax on the thread is holding the chosen card as you reach forward with the left hand and touch the card on the table asking for the name of the card.

Drop the deck to one side of the card on the table. Your hands are clean. Ask a spectator to turn over the card on the table. As he does so, grasp the thread as shown in #2 and pull down on it. This pulls the selected card up above the open wallet in pocket.

When spectator turns over card on the table and sees it is not his chosen card, smile, show the empty right hand and reach into your breast pocket. It is no trouble to peel the waxed thread off the chosen card and push the card into the wallet.

Remove wallet from pocket, allowing it to fold around properly, and once more you have managed to make a card vanish from the deck and appear in your wallet!

CARD IN MOUTH [*Lee Noble*]

Just before the end of a card routine, light a cigarette and puff on it. Have a card selected, initialed by a spectator and returned to deck. Bring to top of deck. Double-lift and show that it is not on top of the deck. Replace cards on top of deck. Show that face card of deck is not selected card. Put deck behind your back and ask spectator to think of a number between one and ten.

Explain that you are going to attempt to make the selected card appear at the thought of number. Behind your back remove the top card from deck and fold it into eights. Clip the folded card between the base of the middle and ring fingers of the right hand. Bring the deck from behind back in left hand and drop on table. As you place the deck on the table take the cigarette out of your mouth with your right hand (masking the folded card with the curled fingers).

"I shan't touch the cards in any way from this moment on—name the number you thought of—and count down to that number—your card will be at the number you thought of!"

Watch carefully, all your attention focused on the spectator who is counting off the cards. Assume he names eight as the number thought of; as he counts off the seventh card, and is just about to pick up the eighth card, put the cigarette to your mouth and pop the folded card into your mouth behind the screen of your fingers. All attention is on the eighth card.

With the card in your mouth, take a drag on your cigarette and hold a puff of smoke in your mouth. When he turns over the eighth card, it is an anticlimax. His card is not there.

Smile, drawing attention to yourself. Twist your ear with your right fingers and as you do so, blow out a puff of smoke and eject the selected card!

POCKETED [*Paul Curry* and *Bill Woodfield*]

A deck is shuffled by the spectator and spread by the spectator. He takes a card. He puts it back in the spread. He collects the cards and shuffles the deck. He holds the deck and for the first time the magician steps in. While the spectator holds the deck the performer tells him that there is no way that he, the magician, can know the identity of the card under these test conditions. (This, oddly enough, is completely true. The performer has no idea what the card is.)

While the spectator holds the deck the magician takes a card at a time from it, calling off the name of the card. The spectator has been told that the moment his card is named he is to slam his hand down on top of it. The magiciaan merely bends up a corner of a card, names it, and waits. If there is no response from the spectator he takes it. But each time he calls it, he waits, and only when there is no answering slap from the spectator does the magician take the card.

When the magician does call the name of the chosen card the spectator slams his hand down on it. The spectator at this point is told to shuffle his card into the remainder of the cards in his hands, losing it again. The part of the deck that the magician holds is added to this.

Seemingly all the magician knows at this point is the name of a card which is lost in the deck. Actually, he has palmed the card, for this whole elaborate busi ess has just provided a fine cover-up for the palming of a card!

After the spectator has taken his card and shuffled the deck, the performer has to spot the bottom card of the deck. When he lifts the corner of the top card he miscalls this as the bottom card, which he has just spotted. The second card is called by the real name of the first one. The third is miscalled as the second, and so on. When the chosen card is named and the spectator slams his hand down on it, it is not his card. His card is on top of the packet in the magician's hand. The magician palms it and adds the rest of the packet to the packet that the spectator holds.

Carry the palmed card to the right pants pocket. Leave it there and wait while the spectator shuffles the deck. Once he has done so, have him fan the deck and search for his card. It has vanished..

Smile amiably and reach into the tiny watch pocket in the front of your pants and pull out the chosen card. This revelation is one of very few that is strong enough to be paired with this location.

The gimmick? You cut a slit through your right pants pocket up through the base of the watch pocket. Sew neatly and you are all set.

You will find in performing that, as you put the palmed card in your trouser pocket, all you need do is shove it upward with the thumb which sets it in the bottom of the watch pocket.

There is an odd optical illusion involved here. Even while the card is coming from the watch pocket, it looks too big to fit in the pocket from which you are taking it.

CLIP IT [*Garcia*]

Needed are 2 red kings, a black ace, and a paper clip. You'll have to experiment with the clip for a while until you get it adjusted so that it will slip off the card when it should and hold when it should.

Begin by showing the 2 red kings and the ace, holding the cards one on top of the other in the left hand as in Fig. 53, #1. The drawing shows the underside of the cards, the faces are to the spectators. The ace is on top of the little block of 3 cards, as in #2. The ace is removed and placed on the bottom of the

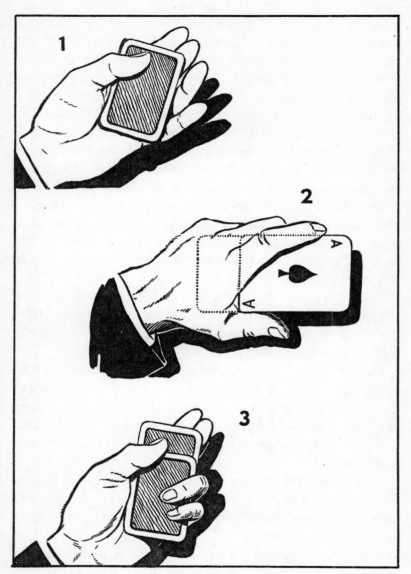

Fig. 53

packet. However, you really use the glide as shown in #2 and #3 to pull back the bottom card which allows you to take off 2 cards as one. The ace has a king hidden behind it when you place it on the bottom.

This move is done a second time. The effect to the audience at this point is that the ace is in the middle of the 3 cards. Fan them backs-up and have the spectator point to the middle card, which he thinks is the ace. When turned over, it is, of course, a king. After some patter the top card is shown to be the ace.

The second phase is like the first, but you only do the glide move once—the first time. The ace is placed on top of the 2 kings, face-up. You glide, placing 2 cards as one under the last card, and the spectators think that the ace is on top when really it is in the middle.

These two phases are just preparation for the clip move. Show the paper clip and explain that since the audience has had trouble in following the ace you will make the problem simpler by placing the clip on the ace.

Hold the ace and one king in the left hand and the other king in the right hand, the paper clip is first placed on the ace and then transferred, unknown to the audience, to the king by means of the move shown in Fig. 54, #1, #2, #3, and #4. The cards dropped on the table and when the clipped card is turned over, it is not the ace.

At this point the real ace is picked up and casually switched for the clipped king, as in #4. The result, when they try to find the ace, is that the clipped card which a moment ago was seen to be a king, is now the ace.

In the fourth phase of the routine the 3 cards are shuffled and one of the kings is miscalled as the ace. The three cards are laid down, face-down, the clipped king and the ace are picked up for a moment, and the move is done, switching the clip to the ace.

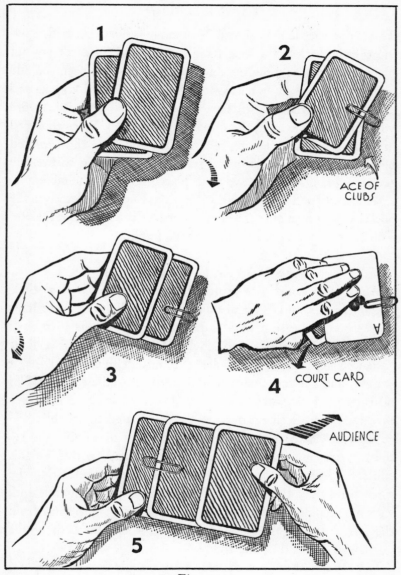

Fig. 54

The clipped ace is then shown. The move is next reversed, moving the clip back to the king from the ace, and the cards are not placed back on the table. Again the spectators have been fooled!

The ace is picked up and switched for the clipped king as you explain that perhaps 3 cards are too confusing (#5). Therefore you eliminate one card, the one bearing the clip. Place this card in your pocket, after having removed the clip. The clip is placed on the ace, the move is made, transferring the clip to the one remaining king, and the two cards placed down on the table.

The unclipped card (the ace) is picked up and placed in the pocket as you turn over the clipped card. It is a king, not the ace. You have now finished "clipping" the public.

FANCY FREE [*A. V. Walsh*]

Audley V. Walsh has explored each facet of magic as thoroughly as he could. Typical of his investigations are these hints on the best and easiest ways to fan cards. Few effects with cards are as pretty as single and double fans. Required is a little patience, some fanning powder ("Faneze," sold at all magic stores), and for these particular designs of Audley's, a deck of cards cut in such a way that one end of the cards are narrower than the other. Such cut decks can be purchased reasonably.

"Faneze" each card, then reassemble the deck. In Fig. 56, the top drawing shows a standard single fan. To achieve this effect, hold the deck as shown in #1 in the left hand. Bring the right hand over the far end of the deck as shown in #2 and, with a sweeping, swirling motion, rotate your right hand from the left to the right, applying pressure on the far ends of the cards with the ball of the thumb.

For the easiest method of performing double fans (see Fig. 55, circled drawing) cut the deck in half and riffle-shuffle the two packets together after reversing one packet. Since the deck has

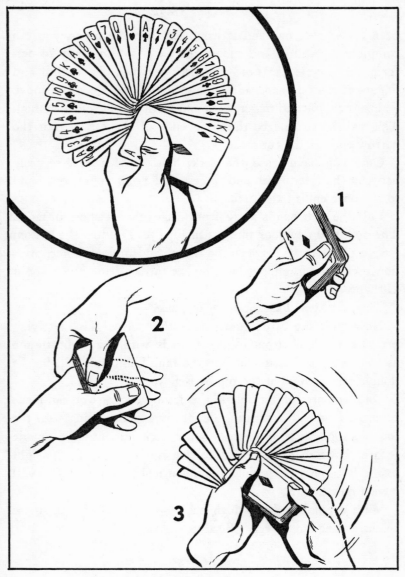

Fig. 55

been cut so that one end is narrower than the other, you can complete the shuffle and square the deck. When ready to perform the double fan hold the deck between the thumb and fingers of the left hand at the outer end of the deck and move your left thumb and fingers back and forth in a beveling motion. This will serve to free the wide ends of the cards from the narrow ends of the cut cards.

Once you have freed the deck, hold the far ends securely between the left thumb and fingers and bring your right hand to the near end of the deck.

Pull the two hands away from each other a short distance. The deck will now look like #1 in Fig. 56. Holding the bottom section of the cards between the thumb and middle finger, press down with the forefinger bending the cards a trifle into a slight U-shape.

This bend will lock the cards in place.

Now with the cards bent, make the normal fan, applying pressure to the bottom block of cards with the right thumb as you sweep the cards out into the fan. The result will be the double fan pictured at the top of Fig. 56.

Once you are comfortable in this fanning action you can make eccentric fans with a pleasing design by experimenting with the top block of cards. Try pulling the deck out into the double length shown in #1 and then forcing the top block to the right or the left at a 45 degree angle. Then make your fan. You will have a new design.

With a fanning deck which has a special back design, these eccentric fans can be very effective.

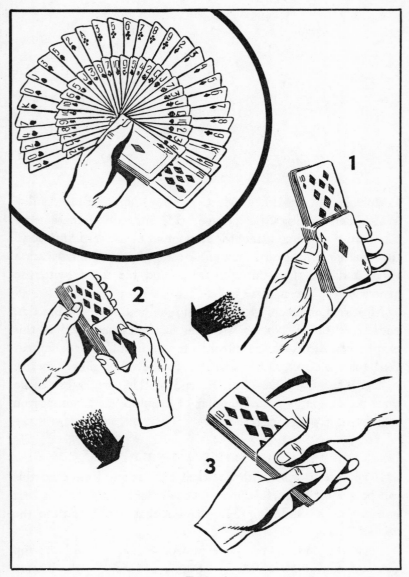

Fig. 56

CHAPTER 6
♥ ♣ ♦ ♠

The "Expert" at the Card Table

Performers like Mickey MacDougall, John Scarne, Audley Walsh, and Francis Carlyle have made enviable reputations by their ability to demonstrate the stratagems of the card "hustler," the "mechanic," the card cheat. Few things have more fascination to an audience than this glimpse behind the scenes with the gentry of the green baize table.

Most real gamblers' sleights require tedious hours of practice, endless rehearsal. Not so with the subtleties described in this chapter. In each case the effect to the audience is that of great skill, but the effect, as you will see, is achieved by simple means.

The "Ten Card Deal" at the end of this chapter can make your reputation as a card-handler of exquisite skill, yet, as you will learn, it works itself!

THE SLIP FALSE CUT

If you are to work with a stacked deck at any time (and this can be a most powerful device) you will need a false cut that is completely convincing. Here is one that will fool even the wariest.

Place the deck on the table in front of you. Hold the top block of cards between the left thumb and fingers, the bottom block between the right thumb and middle finger (Fig. 57, #1). Pull the top block to the right about an inch as in #1.

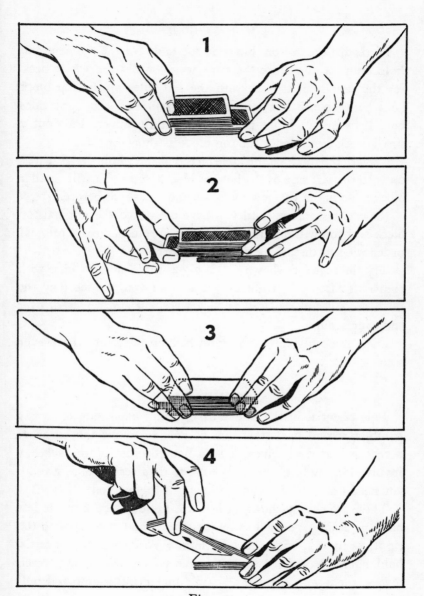

Fig. 57

Disregard the bottom block on the table for the moment and hold onto the top block the same way you did the whole deck, for the first step, that is, with the left sides of the top block held between the left thumb and fingers, and the right sides held between the right thumb and middle finger. Pull out a small block from under the top block as shown in #2.

Replace the block on the table on top of the whole deck squared up with the left side of the bottom block. Pull out a still smaller block from under the new top block and replace as before.

Repeat this process until you have exhausted the original top block and you will find the deck has been returned to its original order without disturbing any of the cards.

Try the sequence shown in #1-2-3-4, three or four times with the cards face-up in front of you so that you can see how the cards are cut and replaced as they were, cut and replaced, over and over again.

Done smoothly this is the most baffling false cut I have ever seen.

SECOND DEAL

It is essential in the course of my bluff exposition of how a gambler second deals that you be able to mimic the action of a real second deal. Since you do not (because of the subtlety involved in my bluff method) have to do a real second deal, all you need learn is the rough mechanics of the method.

These are clearly shown in Fig. 58. Hold the deck in the left hand in dealing position as in #1. Push the top 2 cards to the right, as in #2, with the left thumb. When the top 2 cards, held as one, have been pushed as far as is shown in #3, reach toward them with the right, middle finger and thumb and pull out the second card down with the right fingers, as you pull the top card back into position with the left thumb.

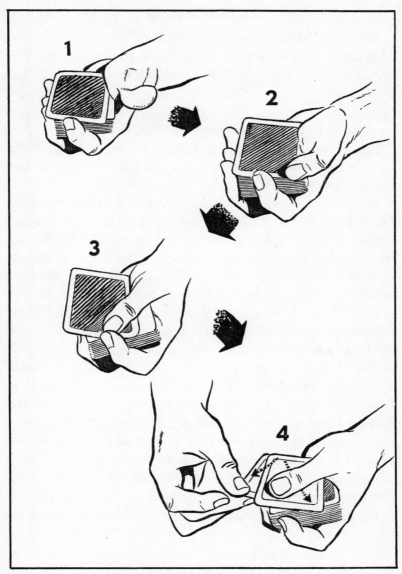

Fig. 58

The arrows show this double movement.

In action, demonstrate this method very slowly, claiming you ordinarily do it very rapidly, so rapidly the action cannot be-detected.

NO SECOND DEAL

I have devised a method of faking a second deal which will get you the same accolades as Scarne and his brethren reap for their hard-earned skill.

Needed is the ability to do an imitation of the second deal. Needed is some brass. Needed is one duplicate card in a deck. Ready? Place, let's say, an ace of clubs, 6 down from the top of the deck. Five cards deeper than this, place the duplicate ace of clubs. The set-up is: 5 indifferent cards, an ace of clubs, four indifferent cards, and another ace of clubs.

Hold the deck in second-dealing position. Turn the top in-different card on the deck face to you and miscall it as the ace of clubs. You patter, "This is the way a crooked gambler op-erates. He has spotted . . ." look at the top card and miscall it, ". . . the ace of clubs on top of the deck and wants to keep it for his own hand." Don't pause here for anyone to ask to see the card but immediately go into a normal deal. After you have dealt out 3 or 4 cards you pause and say, "You see, the second deal exactly—and I do mean exactly—imitates a normal deal." Deal off the next 2 cards and turn the ace of clubs face up to show that you have managed to "retain" it by means of the "second deal."

Leave the cards you have dealt off on the table, and, showing the ace of clubs, drop it face down on top of the deck and again deal. This time they have seen the ace, which removes any sus-picion of the first time when you cheated a little.

"I'll deal a little more slowly than I would ordinarily and let's see if you can catch me . . ."

Deal slowly, but legitimately, again. The ace they have just seen goes face down on the table and you deal 5 cards off on top of it.

"See anything wrong?" you ask as you turn over the second ace of clubs on top of the deck. The audience must admit that your "second deal" is perfection itself.

Put the ace they have just seen to one side, and pick up the packet of 5 cards you have dealt off on the table. This has an ace at the bottom of it, with 5 indifferent cards on top of it. Drop this packet on the deck and pick up the visible ace. Show it and drop it on top of the deck.

(What is happening is that, each time you deal, you are setting up the cards for the next deal.)

Now you can again show the ace on top of the deck, turn it face down, deal off and show the other ace when you come to it.

This can be repeated ad nauseam. I hope you will be able to tell from your audience's attitude when it's time to call a halt.

When you feel that your audience has been "second dealt" to death, change what you have been doing. Assume that the situation now is that you have an ace on top of the deck, followed by 5 indifferent cards and then the ace.

This time deal out the cards as though for a poker hand. The first ace goes to your left, then the indifferent cards; the second one you deal to yourself. Turn it over and show that if you had been playing stud poker, you would have had the advantage of an ace in the hole.

Just show the face of the ace, then drop it on top of the ace to your left and drop these 2 cards onto the other cards on the table as you scoop them up and replace all of them on top of the deck.

Now the situation is that you have an ace, ace, on top of the deck. I once ended the routine at this point by double-lifting and showing the ace, and replacing the double-lift on the bottom of the deck. The spectators see an ace of clubs on the bottom of the deck, which means that after a pause you have wonderful cover for a bottom palm. I used to bottom palm the ace of clubs and drop it in my pocket, turning the deck over face-up, spreading the cards on the table as I did so. This was clean because the other ace of clubs was still there, as silent proof that nothing had happened.

Here is an alternative ending:

Have the duplicate ace on top of the deck. Say, "Besides a second deal, most 'hustlers' also are very expert at palming." Saying this, do a palm off the top of the deck, grabbing the top ace with the right hand. Remove the hand and turn the palm up to reveal the ace.

"Many gamblers, once they have held out a good card, like this one, leave it in their laps until they need it again." You go through the motion of leaving it on your knee. "Some, under the excuse of reaching for a cigarette or for money, leave it in their pocket." You suit the action to the word, but leave the card in the pocket. Your hand comes out empty, but held a little crampedly as though still palming the card.

"Their next problem arises when they want to replace the held-out card on the deck." Your empty hand, which you pretend conceals a card, comes down over the deck. "A good replacement is very important. —There, did you catch any movement? No? Good." You turn over the top card and show the ace. Finis.

To the audience you have demonstrated an absolutely perfect second deal under test conditions. You have palmed a card and replaced it perfectly.

Try this. I think you'll agree it can highlight any pseudo-gambling exposé.

THE EASIEST BOTTOM DEAL

A true, two-handed bottom deal is one of the most difficult of the gamblers' stratagems to do correctly and invisibly. For the purposes of demonstration, however, this little-known, one-handed bottom deal is most effective, most baffling, and seems to require much more skill than it really employs.

A real gambler's move, it was originally invented for occasions where two gamblers work as confederates. It is used rarely and only when the dealer is sitting to the left of his confederate. In such a case, he will bring 2 aces to the bottom of the deck and in the course of dealing legitimately from the top of the deck to the other players, will use this move, just twice, to throw the aces to his partner.

Hold a deck in the ordinary dealing position except that it is a little higher, a little lifted from the palm as shown in Fig. 59, #1. By beveling the cards a trifle and pressing the bottom joint of the forefinger gently against the bottom card, peel it free and allow the bottom card to fall from the bottom of the deck so it rests against your palm, free of the deck.

Don't try to throw the loose bottom card from your hand; instead, pull the hand back from the card. Its own inertia will cause it to drop from your hand onto the table.

If you try to catapult the card from your hand you will defeat the action and make what should be a graceful, deceptive move, a clumsy, obvious artifice.

Once you have released the first card, repeat the sequence again and again, allowing the bottom card to drop, pulling your hand back from the card, and so on.

A rhythm will be developed, and once you have this—release (#2), pull back, drop (#3), release (#4), pull back, drop (#5), established, the move will become quite natural.

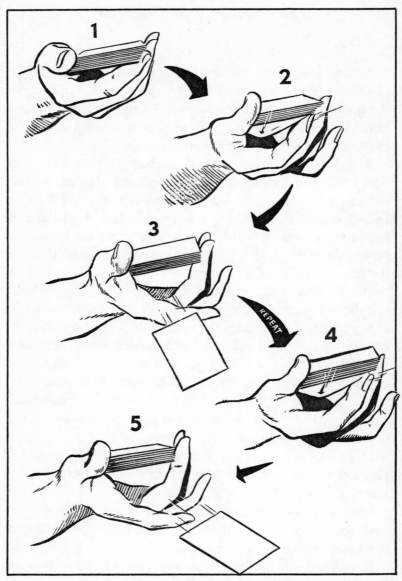

Fig. 59

At one point I was able to do this with a half pack in each hand (which is easier than it sounds) allowing of a seemingly impossible trick.

Have 2 cards selected and bring them to the top of the deck. Cut the deck in half, slipping the top card off the top packet of cards onto the top of the bottom packet of cards.

You are all set. You can now proceed to bottom deal with both hands, asking each of the spectators to say "stop" at a different point. Bottom deal until told to stop by the first spectator. Allow him to take off the top card of the packet, his card, and continue bottom dealing with the other packet until told to stop.

Have the second spectator remove the top card from this packet and you have performed quite a trick!

TABLE-CUT

The standard pass is difficult enough when the performer is standing and able to mask the movements of the cards by bodily movements. It becomes almost impossible to reverse a cut (which is all a pass does) when seated at a table, as in so many card tricks or as in the course of a demonstration of gambler's sleights.

And yet the question is asked again and again: "What does the gambler do after he has brought the cards he wants to the top or the bottom of the deck and the deck is cut?"

The purpose of the cut, of course, is to lose the top and bottom cards. Since the standard pass is out at the table, many methods have been devised to reverse the cut *on* the table.

My method has the merit of being easy of execution; as a matter of fact, it is easier than any other I know. The deck is on the table. A spectator has just cut it into two parts. A true cut would replace those two parts so that what was the top block of cards would go to the bottom, and the bottom block would become the top block.

A false table-cut does the opposite; it brings the deck back to its original position, just as it was before the cut. I accomplish this by pushing the top card of the bottom block off the block slightly, as shown in Fig. 60, #1. The hand comes down over the block and, as it does so, the fingers press against the top card, pushing it off the block and tilting it slightly as shown.

Using this pushed-off card as a scoop, I bring the block up into my thumb crotch as my fingers reach out for the other block as in #2.

In #3 this action is shown with the hand removed.

The outstretched finger tips reach across the near block towards the far block and bring the two blocks together (#4). This would be difficult of accomplishment were it not for the fact that the single, pushed-off card acts like a knife and allows the block of cards below the pushed-off cards to be pushed under the other block of cards.

The hand then squares up the complete pack and the cards are back in their original position.

The whole action is performed in a split second while you are pattering about what you are going to do with the deck.

The sequence is: Spectator cuts the deck, you reach for the near block of cards, push off the top card, use it to get under the other block of cards, and use the thumb and fingers to pull the two blocks together into a unit.

The fact that you are using one hand for this while you fidget with some chips, or gesture with the other hand, is enough to make the audience relax its attention for the infinitesimal bit of time you need to reverse the cut.

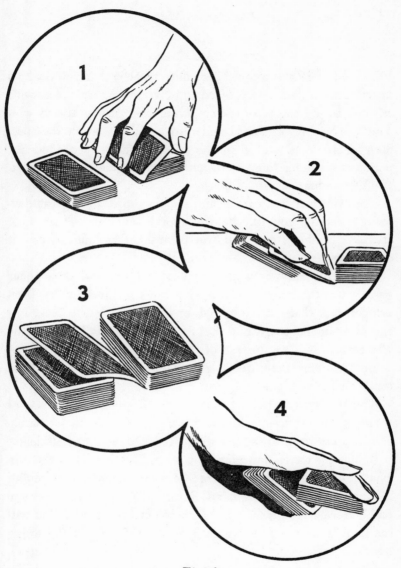

Fig. 60

TEN CARD DEAL

The effect of this astonishing poker stunt is that you deal 10 cards out of a deck and proceed to play two-handed poker with anyone. In the course of showing your control you always win. You win when you shuffle and deal. You win when the spectator deals. You win when the spectator deals, second deals, peeks, changes his mind as to what card to give you. In short, you win under every condition!

You win over and over again, seeming to display great dexterity. Really, you can be the most un-nimble fingered of frenzied fumblers and still win because of an underlying bit of subtlety.

Originally this was a method used for the end of a poker game when there are only two winners. The "hustler" has been using a deck that has ten bowed, or long cards in the deck. For the clean-up he strips out the 10 cards and can then do the effect which follows. Instead of cut cards, deal out 3 sets of 3 of a kind. Assume they are: 3 tens, 3 queens, and 3 kings. The tenth card is an eight (Fig. 61).

The tenth card, the eight which matches none of the sets of three, is the gimmick! I know of few effects in which such a big result comes from so small a secret. It is the height of efficiency.

Shuffle the cards as much as you want. Cut them, mix them in a hat if you so desire. Just be sure that the opponent gets the eight. You will get the winning hand. Before you will believe this you had better get 10 cards and deal them out for a while. You will see that, as sure as fate, whoever gets the eight gets the losing hand!

Now for presentation. It doesn't take a card expert to shuffle 10 cards and run the 9 from the top to the bottom of the packet and then from the bottom to the top. You can peek to learn

Fig. 61

where the eight is and shuffle in such wise that it winds up on top of the packet. You can have it on top of the packet to begin with and overhand-shuffle, retaining the eight on top. You can have it on top and milk-shuffle, peeling the top and bottom cards off 2 by 2. In other words, there are many methods by which you can make sure that the spectator gets the eight.

Assume you have shuffled the packet and have the eight on top of the packet. Deal, and of course the opponent gets the eight. As you deal off, you know that you will hold the winning hand. The peculiar thing about this effect is that you never know what hand you or your opponent will hold till the cards are turned over. All you know is that you will win. You will find that the spectator can get two pairs and you will get a higher two pair. If he gets the highest two pair, you will have three of a kind, etc.

Shuffle and deal as above a few times showing how you always win. Next, shuffle the eight to the bottom of the packet and give the packet to the spectator. This means that the spectator can deal and still you win. You win because the eight is on the bottom and this goes to the dealer.

Take the packet back, shuffle, keeping the eight on top of the deck and then, for the last shuffle, run another card on top of it, making it second from the top.

This means that you can give the packet to the spectator and, once he had dealt the top 2 cards (giving himself the eight), you can arrange almost any presentation. One good way is this. He has dealt the top 2 cards. (He is a dead duck already but doesn't know it yet.) Now you can tell him he is a Gaylord Ravenal, the notorious Mississippi gambler, that he can second deal, and that the deck is marked. Since the deck isn't really marked and since he can't really second deal he can get the same effect by looking at the top card as he deals and making up his mind as to whether to give it to you or himself. (This, in effect, is the second deal.) Even under these conditions, with him deciding what cards to give you and himself, he still loses!

Keeping the rest of the deck to your left, you can allow the spectator to shuffle legitimately and then deal. This is arranged by your throwing the packet of 10 cards onto the rest of the deck with the eight at the bottom of the packet. Now pick off 9 cards as 10 and allow the spectator to shuffle the cards. When he has finished shuffling and cutting, just take the packet from him and drop it on top of the deck and hand him the deck. This has added the Jonah card, the eight, to the bottom. When he deals he gets the eight as the last card! This is really flabbergasting for seemingly you have had nothing to do with the cards at all.

After having done the effect over and over again you can astound the spectator by having an ace on top of the deck. Then, as above, drop the ten cards onto the deck, pick off 9 as 10, have the spectator shuffle and, while he is shuffling, switch the order of the top 2 cards of the deck so that the ace is on top.

Add the ace to the 9 cards, shuffling the ace to the top of the packet. Hand the packet to the spectator and allow him to look at the cards before he deals them to you. He looks at the top card, sees an ace, figures it must be good for his hand and so gives it to himself and deals you the next card. This means that he has given himself the Jonah card of his own volition!

The variants for the effect seem endless. I haven't attempted to give credit where it is due, for everyone I know has had a hand in the above presentation, from Vernon to Curry, from Martin Gardner who started the whole thing by showing it, to Scarne and Audley Walsh.

I have seen few cards stunts in years that are as much fun to fool with, for you will find as you present it that new ideas keep occurring, that you will more or less make it up as you go along.

Get out the deck. You're on your own!

TAKE TEN [*John Murray*]

"Ten Card Deal" involves 3 sets of 3 of a kind and a tenth card. The trick involves dealing the 10 cards to a spectator and to yourself, so that whichever of you gets the tenth card (the Jonah) will hold the losing hand in poker. Here is a new idea. After you have done the "Ten Card Deal" in any of the various ways already given, you work up to the climax. For the climax show 10 coin envelopes. Have them looked at and have the spectator shuffle the 10 cards. While he is doing this all you have to do is nail-mark one of the envelopes.

Prior to this you have slightly crimped the Jonah card, or ink-marked it, or used whatever identifying marks suits you best. At the end of the spectator's shuffle have him spread out the 10 cards face-down on the table.

The only thing you have to do is pick up the Jonah card and insert it in the nail-marked envelope—"just to show the spectator what you want him to do." Don't bother to seal the envelope, as this will take too much time. Just fold the flap in.

Throw this envelope on the table and have the spectator or spectators (to speed it up) insert the face-down cards in the other 9 envelopes.

The conditions are fantastic. Here are 10 cards that have been shuffled, have been inserted into envelopes so that you cannot know the location or identity of any of them—and yet——

You can have the spectator mix in any way—you can have them thrown into a hat and mixed up—and yet, to bring the trick to a successful climax, all you have to do is to be sure the spectator gets the nail-nicked envelope!

You can take the envelopes out of the hat one by one and, holding them to your forehead, go through a big mental turmoil over whether to give the envelope to the spectator or to yourself.

Or they can be spread out on the table and the spectator allowed to choose 5 envelopes. If the marked envelope is one of the 5 chosen, you should have no trouble in forcing one of the 5. If the nicked envelope is not one of the chosen 5, say, "We'll discard these and use *these*" (the remaining 5).

The ending is up to you and the way you work but, given this set of conditions, the effect is tremendous.

Since this is the climax of the routine, build it even further by offering a ten-dollar bill to the spectator if he gets a better hand than you do. This is certainly as sure a bet as a one horse race!

CHAPTER 7
♥ ♣ ♦ ♠

Mind Reading Is Easy

The success of Dr. Jaks and Dunninger proves, if proof be needed, that audiences are hungry for performances that seem to demonstrate superhuman extra-sensory powers.

In this chapter you will learn how you, too, can seem to read minds, transmit thoughts, even force the dead to obey your commands. In short, you "prove" that you are a man of singular endowments!

500 LTD. [*Greer Marechal*]

The mental magnate offers his audience the choice of one of several books of various sizes. Having selected the book, he hands it to one member of the audience and suggests that the rest of the audience help select a page number. To this end, 3 people each call out one digit and the 3 are put together to form the page number.

The spectator holding the book opens it to that page and notes the first word (or the last word, or the picture on that page, or the word that lies at the sum of the digits in the page number).

And what do you think? That's right, the magician knows what that word is, so that he can either read the man's mind or can use his knowledge to make a prediction—or even, with luck and diligence, use it as a force.

Here's what happens. Pay attention to the patter. The whole secret is in what you say, so say it right.

You have 3 books of various sizes ready to use. One of these is *the* book and must have between 550 and 600 pages (preferably close to 550). The other two are different colors and different sizes—either as to thickness or shape.

Pick up the 3 books and offer them to some member of the audience. Hold the 3 books in a kind of fan with the 550-page book in the center—that is, in one hand hold the 550-page book and another, and in the other hand, hold the remaining book. Say to the spectator, "We want to eliminate a couple of these. Would you point to two books, please?" If he points to the 2 outside books, throw them down and hand him the 550-page book. If he points to any other two, throw the third one aside and ask him to pick one of the remaining two. If he picks the 550-page book, hand it to him. If he picks the other odd book, throw it aside and hand the 550-page book to another spectator. In other words, you force the 550-page book by the standard one-out-of-three force.

I suggest handing the 550-page book to another spectator if the first "eliminates" the other 2, as a means of ruling out the possibility that the man who did the pointing out might say he wanted to use one of the others if you try to hand him his "choice."

But that's beside the point. Force the 550-page book any way you please or, if you want to, start out with just the one book.

The magician shows the "selected" book and flips through its pages as he talks. From here on, he says the following as casually as possible:

"This book has about, let's see, 550 pages. Now what we want to do is select just one of these pages. But so we all can have a chance to participate in this experiment—and of course, to rule out the possibility there might be any collusion between this gentleman and myself—let's do it this way. Let's have 3 people each call out a number, just one digit, and we'll put the 3 digits together for our page number.

"Of course, that will limit us to pages over 100, if we use 3 digits. But I think it is better to have the 3 people helping . . . and, since there are 550 pages in the book, that still leaves us with 450 some odd possibilities, which ought to be enough to rule out coincidences, don't you think?

"I'll ask three of you to call out a number, and, oh yes, since there are only 550 pages in the book, we won't need numbers over 5. That will give us every combination from 100 to 555, which ought to be enough, don't you think—455 possibilities?

"Here we go: Will you, sir [pointing to any spectator], give me the first number under 5 that you think of? Thank you. Now you [point to another], will you call out *another* number under 5? Thank you. Now, one more, would you [pointing to another], give me *another* number under 5? Thank you."

And that's the essence of the secret—more or less. If you followed the above suggested patter, you will note that the 550 pages in the book were mentioned several times. Also, several other numbers were bandied about to an extent that the audience probably will not follow. Usually, if an audience can't follow what it believes to be incidental palaver, it will accept what you say as fact rather than going to the trouble to work it out. So when you make the obvious misstatement that eliminating all digits over 5 will give you every combination between 100 and 555, no one will challenge the remark.

The point is that you dull their perception with what they think is unnecessary prattle and then spring the gag when they are unsuspecting.

But you're not through the skullduggery yet. After having sold the fact that you're going to eliminate all digits over 5 ask for the people to call out digits *under* 5. They won't quarrel with you—really. You see, after saying not to use numbers over 5, you suddenly pounce upon some unsuspecting spectator and demand a number under 5. He gives you one. You ask 2 others to give you the *other* numbers under 5, and you move right along—not even stopping to breathe. If you can build up a rather hectic haste (hectic, not guilty) during the number calling, you'll find that you'll be well into the next part of the trick before anyone stops to realize what has happened.

Three digits have just been called out. Since the patter outlined has eliminated zeros, all digits over 4, and all repeats, the only answers you can possibly get are 1, 2, 3, or 4. Three of these have been chosen. After the third, you say, "All right, the digits that were chosen were 1, 2, and 3 (or whatever they were). Will you please look on page 123 of the book?"

In other words, whatever 3 of the 4 possible digits were called out, you repeat them *arranged in ascending order, regardless of the order in which they were called out.* Thus, if 4, 1, and 3 were selected in that order, you say, "The digits that were chosen were 1, 3, and 4."

Think about that and you will see that there are only four possible page numbers that can be arrived at (123, 124, 134), and 234) out of an original 455 possibilities. By eliminating zeros, repeats, all digits over 4, and anything but ascending order of digits, all but 4 combinations have been eliminated.

That's all. You can read their minds by knowing the first word on the only 4 pages that can be chosen. You can make a prediction on a piece of paper and switch for the proper one of 4 slips in your pocket; you can use a medium assistant and only have to cue her one of 4 words, or—and this is intriguing—you can keep looking until you find a book that has the same word in the first or last place on pages 123, 124, 134, and 234 and you'll have a force to end all forces.

A quick summary:
1. Force book with 550 pages.
2. Plug 550 pages and say you will eliminate numbers over 5.
3. Call for numbers *under* 5.
4. Arrange in ascending order.
5. Have word noted.

Whatever denouement you use, you will probably want to recapitulate what has happened by remarking that one of several books was chosen and that 3 people helped choose the page in that book in such a way that, not only couldn't you know what was selected, but the spectators themselves couldn't know what would come up.

Incidentally, if you use the digits 1, 2, 3, 4, and 5 and a book with 660 pages, you'll have only 10 possibilities to contend with.

CLIP COLOR [*Walter Gibson*]

Novelty in effect or method is the prime requisite for mental effects—here is one providing both. It is more than an adaptation of earlier ideas, for it carries a new twist.

The magician introduces four cards, each of a different color, red, yellow, blue and green, along with 4 small envelopes of the drug variety. He intends to put the cards in the envelopes but, since the cards are too large, he uses a pair of scissors to cut them up.

Here, by way of variety, he cuts them differently. The red card is cut into 4 pieces, the blue into 6, the yellow is snipped into 8 segments and the green cut into a full dozen. These fragments are given to different persons, each receiving an envelope as well. In this way the clipped cards are sealed away from view.

However, these persons are told to choose a certain color, which is sealed last. More than that, they must count the pieces before putting them away so that all minds will be concentrated upon that one color and the number associated with it. This, of course, is done while the performer's back is turned.

Gathering the sealed envelopes, the magician explains that he is going to spell to the thought. For example, he says to a spectator, "Your name is George. If we were using it, we would spell G-E-O-R-G-E, putting an envelope at the bottom of the heap until the final letter. That would be your envelope since it would represent your name."

Now comes the real mystery. Giving the envelopes to any spectator, the magician has the latter shuffle them thoroughly and return them. Spreading the envelopes to show them all alike, the magician asks what color was chosen. When told, he closes the fanned envelopes and hands them to the speller *without the slightest false move.* Yet, when the spell is made and the final envelope opened, inside are found the pieces of the chosen color!

Read the following carefully and the secret will be apparent.

Though clipped carelessly, the cards *must* be cut into the numbers given: red—4, blue—6, yellow—8, and green—12. The envelopes are given out with the cards. Each envelope has a tiny crayon mark on the lower left corner, on the back. Make it a dot so small that only you will notice it. One color, of course, can be eliminated; preferably yellow, as its absence will tell the color.

The cut cards go in the proper envelopes, which are sealed. In spelling the name in the demonstration, the magician turns the envelopes *backs down*, for a reason to be given later. After a shuffle, however, he turns them *backs up*, to spread and remarks that they are all alike. A cute point this, for while emphasizing it, the magician notes the tiny dots, when asking for the name of the color chosen.

Suppose *red* is named. If the red envelope is at position 3 or 4, simply hand over the envelopes. For position 3, you tell the spectator to spell red. For position 4, you ask—as though you didn't know—how many red pieces there were. When the spectator says "four," you tell him to spell it.

Should *red* be at position one or 2, you merely *turn over* the envelopes when handing them to the speller. Quite logical, because the envelopes were *face up* when you explained the "George" spelling earlier. This will change the positions of one or 2 into 3 or 4, respectively, and you simply give the business of spelling "red" or "four" as the case requires.

For *blue* you do the same as red, remembering only that the color spelling applies to position 4, and the spelling of the pieces (6 in this case) applies to position 3. A few trials will show how easy, in fact how automatic the whole thing is.

If anything, the 2 remaining colors are easier. For position one—you have a person spell *green*. For position 2—emphasize the number *twelve*, and have him spell it. Positions 3 and 4 require a turnover, four becoming position one (*green*) and three becoming position 2 (*twelve*).

In turn, positions one and 2 are already set for *eight* or *yellow*, and by the simple process of turning the envelopes face up, you take care of positions 4 and 3, making the spellings *eight* and *yellow*.

No need to memorize all this. Do the trick deliberately, which makes it more effective, and in the course of so doing you will have no trouble with the process.

Mind Reading Is Easy

phoney [*Alan Barnert*]

At a party or similar gathering the performer demonstrates the "mind-reading" ability of an absent acquaintance of his by having a card chosen; the mind reader announces the chosen card—and then repeats this performance with two more cards.

Three different methods are used for the three cards. The whole effect is a routine of some new and some old methods. The complete effect and methods will be presented in the form of a play, since this seems to be the clearest way of describing all the actions and patter which together form the routine.

CAST OF CHARACTERS

Joe Bloke, the performer; Ed Niles, the "mind reading" confederate (alias John Charelle); Anne, Bea, Charley, Dick, four of the spectators; Other spectators.

PROLOGUE

Scene: Ed Niles' apartment. His preparation for the act has consisted of the following: He has read these instructions and run through them several times with Joe Bloke. He has a sheet with the various data typed on it in his desk drawer. (This sheet will be described and the data listed later.) Otherwise he is unprepared. He has no codes to remember and does not yet know that the effect is to be worked this evening. He is in the apartment.
Time: Any. (The phone rings. Ed answers.)

Ed. Hello.

Joe. (Who has called to put the machinery in motion.) Is that you, Ed? Do you expect to be home tonight?

Ed. Yeah. What's up? (*Note:* It is not necessary that Ed be at home later, as long as he can be reached by phone.)

Joe. I figure on working "Phoney" tonight at about ten. I'll be at Academy 2-2222. Check?

Ed. Let me write that down. Ten o'clock, Academy 2-2222. (He writes this information and leaves it near the phone. He then locates the data sheet and also keeps it handy. He has no other duties until he is called again at ten o'clock.)

PART 1

Scene: An apartment in the same city that night just before ten o'clock. There is a gathering of some sort at which JOE proposes to work "Phoney." During the last few minutes he has guided the conversation around to the subject of spiritualism, mind reading, etc. There is a telephone in the room, whose number he previously gave to ED. (Assume he is prepared for all three parts of this trick, although some of it will be unintelligible on the first reading. First he has called ED to make sure that ED will be available and where—and to tell him the phone number from which the effect will be worked.

Second, he has with him a specially prepared address book, with the same data in it as are on ED's sheet. Third, he has memorized a short code for the third card. Fourth, he has learned the routine with ED.)

JOE. (Continues conversation with spectators) in fact I know of a fellow named John Charelle.* If we think of any card at all and call him at Atwater 7-2345, he'll be able to read our minds and tell us the card. At least I've seen him do it before. Say Anne, call him up. Here's his number . . . (Writes this number, which is, of course, ED's, on a slip of paper and leaves it in sight.)

JOE. . . . ask for John Sharelle. Now let's pick a card; we don't need a deck for that—suppose two or three of you name cards and we'll vote on one of them . . . (This is done and the three of diamonds is picked. This choice is honest and any other method, of course, could be used.)

JOE. . . . All right, Anne, now that we've chosen a card, suppose you get a deck so that we can get a look at the three of diamonds to get a good picture of it in our minds. (ANNE goes to get a deck.)

JOE. . . . In the meantime let me check that number just to make sure . . . (He looks at the slip on which he has written ED's num-

* *Editor's Note:* Author has deliberately used alternative spellings of name throughout, to illustrate the simplicity of working the code.

ber, then looks through the address book which he takes from his pocket.)

Joe. . . . Yes, that's right, John Shorel—Atwater 7-2345 . . . (Writes the name above the previously written number.)

Joe. . . . Anne, do you have the deck now. Give it to me, please. (Takes deck, fans it face up, removes three of diamonds, and places it on table for everyone to gaze at. He also starts to prepare for the second part by doing the following. He locates the ten of diamonds in the face-up fan. In closing the fan he cuts the ten to the bottom of the pack. He turns cards face down, lays pack, with ten on top, on table. Purpose is to be able to locate the ten later. Any maneuver such as jog or crimp could also be used.)

Joe. . . . All right, if everyone has seen the card and pictured it in his mind, Anne, pick up the card yourself and call John. (Anne picks up card, goes to telephone, checks number and dials it.)

Ed. Hello.

Anne. I'd like to speak to Mr. John Scharrelle.

Ed. Who?

Anne. Mr. John Schorel.

Ed. Sorry, Miss. I still can't make out that name. Will you spell it, please?

Anne. S C H A R R E L L E

Ed. Oh, Mr. Schorel. He lives upstairs. I'll call him. (What he actually does is to consult the data sheet. There are many ways of spelling *Shirel* and 52 of them are listed on the sheet, each corresponding to a card. The name was not written down until after the card was chosen and, of course, the appropriate spelling was used. When Anne reads the name off she automatically codes the card.)

Ed. (returns to phone) This is Mr. Shurrel. Who is this?

Anne. We understand that you can read minds.

Ed. Oh, you are thinking of something, are you? Wait a minute, let me think. It is a card, a red card (etc., etc. . . .) the three of diamonds. Is that right?

Anne. That's right!

Ed. Now wait a minute, don't hang up. That one was too easy. I can sense Joe Bloke is there with you and he has a very easy mind to read. Let's try again and this time make it harder by not letting Joe knew what card you pick. Take your card, the three of diamonds, and push it into the deck, and then use the card below it. Joe will show you how, but don't let him see the card. Do you understand?

ANNE. I think so.

PART II

Start of Part II: (This will be a force of the ten of diamonds, and again you have your choice of methods. The one JOE uses goes as follows: The deck is lying on the table face down with the ten of diamonds on top. During ANNE's conversation with ED, JOE picks up the deck, cuts it about twelve to fifteen cards from the top and completes the cut, keeping the tip of the left, little finger above the smaller, lower packet. The pack is held this way until ANNE has received the instructions from ED. The pack is held towards her, still in the left hand. The right hand riffles the front, or outer end of the deck for her to insert the card, while the right thumb enlarges and enters the break at the inner end. The riffle starts just above the lower packet so there is no chance of the card being inserted into the lower packet. As soon as the card is inserted, the riffle stops. JOE tells ANNE to hold onto the card, and the right thumb and finger draw off the whole upper packet lengthwise inwardly. This leaves the three of diamonds, still held by ANNE, immediately above the ten, which is the upper card of the lower packet. It appears as though the three had been placed there by ANNE. The lower packet is then pulled away slowly from the three, the upper card pushed sideways by the left thumb and the packet held towards ANNE.)

JOE. I've done this before with John. Take that card, Anne. Show it to everybody else but not to me. Then go back to the phone. I'll leave the room. (ANNE shows the card to everyone while JOE leaves the room. She then goes to the phone where ED goes through the business of telling her that her card is the previously agreed upon ten of diamonds. They hang up and JOHN returns.) *Note:* if by chance the ten of diamonds is chosen as the *first* card, an alternate, say the two of spades is used as the second.

PART III

JOE. John has never told me how he does it or even whether there's a trick to it or not. It seems to be impossible for him to guess a freely selected card by trickery unless someone here told him. I'm sure Anne is not his confederate and she is the only one who spoke to him. Just to make doubly sure, let's try it again and this time we'll eliminate a few loopholes that I've been thinking of. In the first place, we'd better eliminate Anne from this one altogether, so let's have her leave the room before we pick the card. I'm probably suspect too, even though I didn't see the second card and wasn't in the room when it was telepathed or whatever you call it. So I'd better leave the room when you call. Also, this time we'll have whoever calls not know the card himself, so that he can't give any signals in case he, too, is a confederate. Now another thing. I know where John is, but you don't, so he might be across the street looking in here with a telescope. Let's pull the shades down and then he can't see the card we pick. Also, there might be microphones in the walls so that he can hear us name the card after it is chosen. This time let's not name the card at all. Also, we'll use a new method of choosing the card where everybody has a hand in naming the card. I suggest that someone write the name of the four suits on a slip of paper and the names of the thirteen cards of any suit. Then we can all take turns in crossing out either a suit or value until only one suit and one number remain. That will be the card. But if anyone has a different idea, let us hear it . . . (If any different, valid method is proposed, it may be used. The choice this time is honest.)

JOE. . . . Now we also need someone to make the call. Who's the victim this time? (A new subject is chosen by any method.)

JOE. . . . All right, Bea. It seems as if it's you. Now, you're not to know the card, so you and Anne leave the room while we choose one. I'll leave the room before you call. Here's the number I wrote before . . . (Hands her the original slip that ANNE had used.)

JOE. . . . There's one more thing. When you call him up, if he answers himself, don't say a word, not a word. Just dial the number and let him guess the reason for the call. (The shades are drawn, ANNE and BEA leave the room. The suits and values are written on a sheet of paper. At some point in the proceedings prior to this, the phone has rung and someone has answered, but it was the wrong number. In the meantime, the choosing goes forward and eventually a card is chosen. The name is written down so there can be no mistake but the deck is not used at all this time to forestall sleight-of-hand.)

JOE. . . . Charley, will you tell Bea to come in now and make the call and I'll leave . . . (He goes over to the phone and picks up the receiver, handing it to BEA when she comes in.)

JOE. Okay, now all of you think of the card while she calls. (Hands over the phone and leaves. BEA dials the number and ED answers.)

ED. This is Mr. Churelle again, do not say a word. Just do what I say. Motion to everyone to come near the phone so they can get their thoughts across more easily. Hold the earphone away from your ear so everyone can hear me talk . . . (Waits a moment, then shouts so that everyone can hear.)

ED. . . . You are thinking of the *ace of clubs!* (The *wrong number* call was ED calling. He had been given the number earlier in the evening, remember? When someone answered the phone he asked for Dave's Delicatessen or something, and was told that he had a wrong number. *He did not hang up*, however, but kept the receiver to his ear. The connection therefore was not broken but was kept open even though the called phone was hung up. Thus, when JOE picked up the receiver to hand it to BEA, ED heard the words addressed to the assemblage: "Okay, now all of you, etc." This was the code phrase. As soon as he heard it he replaced the receiver, breaking the connection and allowing the dial tone to be heard by BEA. He then had time to look up the code phrase in his book and was ready to announce the card a few seconds later when his phone rang. JOE, of course, has to memorize the code phrases, but they are alphabetical and easy to remember. Only the first few words are part of the code. Those of you who know a similar code already, such as Annemann's, will not have to learn a new one but can use the old, adapting it or the routine if necesaary. The complete data sheet used by ED and, in the form of an address book, by JOE, follows.)

DATA SHEET

PART I

Spades		Hearts		Diamonds		Clubs	
Charel	ace	Chirrel	ace	Scharel	ace	Schirelle	ace
Charell	2	Chirrelle	2	Scharell	2	Schirrel	2
Charelle	3	Chorel	3	Scharelle	3	Schirrelle	3
Charrel	4	Chorell	4	Scharrel	4	Schorell	4
Charrell	5	Chorelle	5	Scharrell	5	Schorelle	5
Charrelle	6	Chorrel	6	Scharrelle	6	Schorrel	6
Cherel	7	Chorrelle	7	Scherel	7	Schorrelle	7
Cherelle	8	Churel	8	Scherell	8	Schurel	8
Cherrel	9	Churell	9	Scherelle	9	Schurell	9
Cherrelle	10	Churelle	10	Scherel	10	Schurelle	10
Chirell	jack	Churrel	jack	Scherrelle	jack	Schurrel	jack
Chirelle	queen	Churrell	queen	Schirel	queen	Schurrell	queen
Chirrel	king	Churrelle	king	Schirell	king	Schurrelle	king

PART II

10 of diamonds (or 2 of spades if 10 of diamonds was first card).

PART III

"Now . . ."	Spades—one word
"Ready now . . ."	Hearts—two words
"All right now . . ."	Diamonds—three words
"All right, ready now . . ."	Clubs—four words

To summarize, then, the first card is coded by the spelling of the name of the called party. The second one is forced and the third is coded by a phrase spoken before the party is called, but while he is still on an open line from a previous call.

Ace	"All of you be ready to think of the card"
2.	"Be ready to think of the card."
3.	"Can you all see the card in your minds?"
4.	"Do you all have the card in your minds?"
5.	"Each of you think of the card."
6.	"Form a picture of the card in your minds."
7.	"Get a good picture of the card in your minds."
8.	"Have a picture of the card in your minds."
9.	"I want every one of you to have a picture of the card."
10.	"Just get a picture of the card in your minds."
Jack.	"Keep the picture of the card in your minds."
Queen.	"Let's all think of the card."
King.	"Make an effort to think of the card."

(The code for the suit forms the introduction to the sentence and the code for the value is the *first letter* of the main phrase. If the phrase itself is forgotten, just count down the alphabet to get the key initial letter.)

TORN CENTER [*Paul Curry*]

Annemann, in one of his excellent mental routines, touched on an idea in connection with the "torn center" billet trick that can be worked as a separate item. It makes possible a quick, effective mental stunt without sleights or glimpses in the cupped hands.

For a complete description of the mechanics of the "Torn Center," see pages 182–5, *Magic as a Hobby*, by the same author.

Mr. Annemann's idea was to draw the usual circle on the center of the paper and explain that it represented a clock face.

The spectator then drew in the hands of the clock to represent whatever time he wished. The paper was torn to bits and burned, and the performer, in the course of the Annemann routine, revealed the chosen time.

The following is an elaboration on the above: Get a small pad and, in advance, prepare each of the sheets by drawing a clock face in the exact center. Make a dot to indicate the center of the clock face, but do not draw in the hands. Place a tiny pellet of wax in the center of the back of the pad and you are all set (Fig. 62, #1).

Tear off one of the sheets and have a person fill in the hands to show any desired time. Without letting you see what time he has indicated, have him fold the paper in half and then in half again.

Take the paper from him and tear it in half and in half again as is usually done in the "torn center" trick. Rest the papers on the back of the pad, on top of the wax, as your free hand goes for the matches (#2). The center portion should be lowermost of these pieces and rest directly on top of the wax so that a little pressure by the thumb will cause it to adhere to the back of the pad (#3).

The matches are tossed to the spectator who lights one while the performer dumps the torn pieces—with the exception of the center portion fastened to the back of the pad—into an ash tray. The pieces are burned, and while this is going on the performer raises the pad with the handless clock on the face sheet toward the spectator, who is asked to make a mental picture of the position of the two hands he drew on the original paper.

The performer, in the meantime, slips his thumb into the folds of the center piece and flips it open to reveal the information he is after (#3–4). The pad is turned over, the fingers hiding the center piece, and the performer draws the hands in

Fig. 62

the position he just noted on the center piece. This second sheet is torn off, placed clock-side down, and the spectator calls aloud the time he selected. The paper is turned up to show that the performer has indicated the same time on his sheet.

DEVICE [*Dr. Jacob Daley*]

Here is one of the cleanest bill or billet moves I've ever seen. Needed is an envelope, any envelope, with a folded bill in it whose serial number you've memorized. Borrow another similar bill and have the spectator fold it with the serial numbers inside, supposedly so that you cannot see the numbers, really so that the borrowed bill matches your folded duplicate.

Take the bill from the spectator with the opening outward as in Fig. 63, #1. Hold it at your finger tips between the middle and ring finger and thumb. Next, as in #2, bring the bill down into the envelope seemingly, but really allow it to separate at the open ends as in #2 so the top edge of the envelope enters the opening.

Push your hand down into the envelope in the direction of the bottom arrow and this action will automatically force the bill up into the finger palm as indicated by the top arrow in Fig. 2.

The action is perfect. The bill is finger-palmed (#3) as your right hand comes away. Proffer the envelope to the person from whom you borrowed the bill and have him seal it. He has seen you *place* his bill in the envelope. He sees a bill in the envelope when he licks the flap and therefore should be astonished when you read off the serial numbers on "his" bill later.

As you can see, this is a utility move which can be used for a switch of either serial numbers or denominations of bills, or for billet readings.

Please, please, just because the actual mechanical moves are

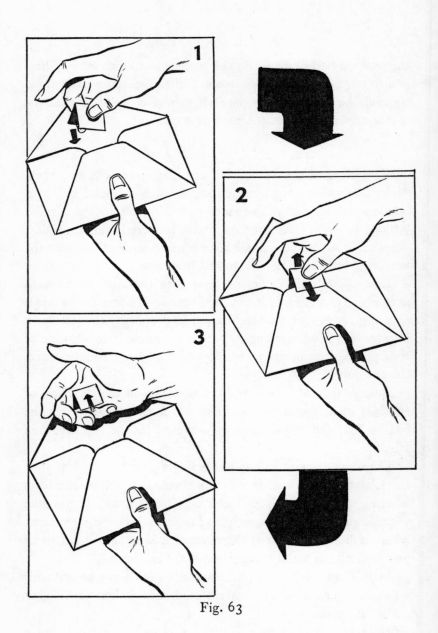

Fig. 63

simple, don't think you can do it without practice. Fool with it until it becomes second nature. Then its true worth will be apparent.

THE MALKIN [*Robert Fairthorne*]

The performer introduces the theme of sympathetic magic in a style suited to himself and to his audience. He instances the by no means extinct practice of molding a wax image around a hair of the intended victim, and then sticking pins in it, in the hope that the prototype will be affected similarly (in some parts of the country the image is named a "malkin," hence the title).

In days of more robust confidence than these, the hope was usually justified, provided the victim knew that the ritual was in operation. But, says the performer, although people are not nowadays so obliging, it is possible to get sympathetic action in trivial matters if this classic technique be followed.

To demonstrate this, he takes two sheets of paper, puts one on the other and cuts from the double sheet the outline of an elementary paper doll, thus creating two malkins—identical twins. The top one he gives to a spectator, along with a thin pencil or wooden skewer. The spectator is told to put the malkin behind his back, crush it, push the skewer through it and then keep everything behind his back so no one can see what he has done. The performer watches these actions intently, with his malkin and a skewer behind his back, explaining that if one keeps one's mind a blank and receives anything one can get (faculties that he had developed since boyhood) it should be possible to duplicate the other's actions exactly.

And so it is, for with his left hand he produces his own malkin from behind his back, and with his right reaches behind the spectator and takes the other malkin from him. When opened out they are found to be similarly perforated.

The under sheet of the two is really a double sheet. The two top edges should be stuck together, best achieved by tearing out two leaves from a pad simultaneously, so that it can be done in sight of all without detection. Thus, when the twin malkins are cut out, they are really triplets, the top one being slid off and given to the spectator. The other two, still superimposed, are crushed and perforated by the performer behind his back while he talks and watches the spectator so intently that some knowing ones will think he is doing visual muscle reading. Also he smooths out his twins, slides them apart into the two hands, and crumples them up again. The left hand throws its malkin on the table, the right goes behind the spectator's back, takes his malkin and throws it under the table (or retains it for future disposal), immediately producing the malkin originally in the hand as the one taken from the spectator. Not unnaturally, they are similarly mutilated. Don't superimpose them to show the exact correspondence! That is merely exposing the trick in reverse.

THE CHINESE PARROT [*Franklin V. Taylor*]

Two cards selected by spectators are placed anywhere in a book. The magician then tells them the names of their cards, the pages at which the cards were inserted, and last, but most definitely not least, he tells them what is on the pages of the book!

For the purpose of the description and Dr. Taylor's patter, I'll describe the effect using two quarter "pocket books." One is Earl Derr Biggers' *The Chinese Parrot* and the other is a John Dickson Carr book titled *The Punch and Judy Murders*. The spectators place their cards in the Punch and Judy Murders. You patter blithely about the super-parrot intelligence of the Chinese Parrot. He is so smart, you insist, that he can read a book through in the twinkling of an eye. While you wait for someone to twinkle an eye, place the Parrot, that is, the book, *The Chinese Parrot*, on top of the other book so the "Parrot" can read it.

If you still have one of those old practical jokes called the "Joy Buzzer," have it under your coat at the breast pocket, all wound and ready to buzz. At the point where the "Parrot" is reading the book, press your arm against the concealed buzzer which goes off with a chatter that *does* sound like a parrot.

This chatter, you say, is the "Parrot" signifying that he has finished reading the book. You are all set for the denouement. The "Parrot" will whisper in your ear the contents of the chosen pages and the names of the chosen cards. All is well, but for one factor. Although the "Parrot" can *read* English, he can't *speak* it. At this dire contretemps you luckily remember your Mandarin. (He is one of those little carved Chinese figures you can buy in any novelty shop.) He will act as translator. Place him on top of the book, *The Chinese Parrot*. The Parrot tells him the necessary information in Chinese and the Mandarin translates the information to you!

This he does in fine style and you retail the contents of the freely chosen pages and the names of the cards to your amused audience.

You don't *have* to use the buzzer or the little figure or the particular books we mentioned. I hope you will, though, because each step has a reason and each little "bit" is just that much more misdirection. The bare bones of the trick resolve themselves down to this.

You need some extra books. You'll need two copies of *The Chinese Parrot* and two of the *Punch and Judy Murders*. Tear off the covers of both "Parrots" and glue them together like a double-backed playing card. You will have a single unit that is a cover on both sides. Read or throw out your two coverless *Chinese Parrots*. The audience never sees them. What they do see are the two *Punch and Judy Murders*.

When you begin, copy (a) of the "Punch" has two force cards in it on certain pages you have memorized.

On top of this cover is the double-backer. To all intents and purposes, you now have what seems to be a copy of "The Chinese Parrot." The other unprepared copy of "Punch" (b) is the one that the poor unsuspecting spectators gently place their forced cards into. (For the force, use a mechanical deck. This is not the kind of trick with which to take chances. Frank recommends the rough and smooth Hull "Nu-Idea" force deck.)

The trick merely requires a bold switch. After the cards go into book (b) give the audience the story about the intelligent parrot. Place the books together so that the "Parrot" can "read" the contents.

Book (a), the fake with the double-sided cover, is resting on your flat, left palm. Book (b) is laid on top of it. The noise of the buzzer startles the audience so that later they don't recall the precise positions of the books. The turn-over comes when you reach for the little statue. Place the statue on top of the now turned over books and all is done. The fake cover is transferred to the other book, and all the mechanics are through. The rest is up to you and your presentation. For, when you take away the now top book, *it* is the one with the force cards in the known pages. The other book, which you place to one side as you listen to the statue, is the book with the double cover on it, for all to see that it is seemingly "The Chinese Parrot."

MORTMAIN [*Stuart Cramer*]

The wizard introduces a shriveled and mummified old hand which he assures his audience is imbued with the spirit of its

former owner. To prove the assertion, he sticks a pencil into
the gnarled relic and holds it in place with a rubber band. Next
he places it gently upon a book, with its title toward the audience. Under the pencil point are thumb tacks and an examined
sheet of paper. Two different books, both ancient ones of course,
are handed out and the magician's calling card is thrust into one
of them by a spectator, to get a page number. Unknown to the
audience there is another card in the same book, at a page the
wizard wants forced. This is as ancient as the word "mortmain"
itself; I give it merely for completeness. Turning the book end
for end, another spectator is requested to open to the place
where the card (the secret one) protrudes, and the page number
is read aloud. Person holding the first book turns to that page
and reads the first word, or line if you wish. This, of course,
is the forced word.

Attention is called to the mummified hand and absolute quiet
is demanded. The magician moves gingerly to the table and
gently strokes the hand, asking it in deep and reverent terms to
give some manifestation of its spirit. He then tiptoes aside, seats
himself facing the audience, and goes into a brown study.

Suddenly the hand moves. Jerkily it writes! The magician
leaps to his feet and rushes to the hand but does not touch it.
He asks the man who selected the word to come forward quickly
and take the paper. Sometimes this individual will decline, but
curiosity usually gets the better of him and he'll take it. Upon
it is written the selected word or sentence.

The book is hollow and contains an electric light bulb. A
lamp on the table provides both a connection and a means of
absorbing any telltale glow from the book. The magician turns
this light on when he last strokes the hand.

Purpose of the light in the book is to provide heat to bring
out the message on the paper, said message having been written

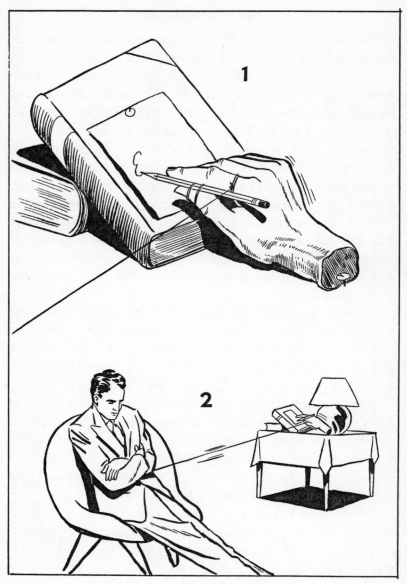

Fig. 64

beforehand in "invisible ink." (Lemon, leek, cabbage juices are some that may be used.)

The hand is moved by means of a thread which is wrapped around a finger of the hand when the pencil is rubber-banded in place (Fig. 64, #1). This thread runs around in back of the book where it is attached to a rubber band which in turn is fastened to the object upon which the book is propped. (A thumb tack in the table, covered by another book is best.) The other end of the thread is picked up by the performer as he moves away from the table to take his seat. With arms folded when he goes into the trance, he manipulates the thread sufficiently to make a few movements of the hand (#2). You'll be surprised at how well the writing motion can be faked with the aid of the back-pull supplied by the rubber band at the other end of the thread. The magician picks up the band at the end of the trick to disengage the thread. He has ample time to do this while urging the spectator to come forward to take the card off the book.

CHAPTER 8

Routined for Deception

In the preceding chapters you have learned a wealth of fine magic. Woven together, any of the tricks in this book can be made into a truly impressive sequence of wonders.

In this last chapter a group of magical inventors have done this weaving process for you and, in the course of so doing, have proved how good magic can be made better with the powers of routining.

I know of no simpler way of getting the effect of producing lit cigarettes from the air than the process described in the first routine, "Out of the Smoke." John Hamilton's routine, called "Bloomin' Silk," shows what can be done with some fairly ordinary silk sleights when they are incorporated into one sequence. Jim Thompson's routine, called "Jocko the Great," called forth plaudits from Dai Vernon who incorporated some of Jim's ideas into his own hand puppet routine. And "Eskow's Act," when first run in my magic magazine, *The Phoenix*, was the single, most popular routine I ever was fortunate enough to be able to print. It was so popular that the issue containing this routine has long been out of print due to demand and I am therefore grateful to be able to run it in these pages. It is too good to have become unavailable.

OUT OF THE SMOKE [*Dave Spindell* and *Clayton Rawson*]

The magician takes a book of paper matches from his pocket (note: paper matches, not a box of matches). The magician attempts to prove his powers. There are no matches in the paper folder. He pantomimes striking an invisible match. Nothing happens. He tries again. Still no result. He closes the match packet, makes a third striking motion up in front of his lips and —he has a lit cigarette in his mouth!

He throws the match packet to one side, exhales a puff of smoke, and produces another cigarette. Then another and another. Four cigarettes in all. This with no body steals, no gadgets, no gimmicks, nothing, seemingly, but his hands.

This routine will do for the start of a regular cigarette routine or may be used as an interlude, and a very baffling interlude at that, between other tricks.

If you can do the thumb palm and if you are willing to take a half hour making three dummy cigarettes, you will have this pretty conceit always at hand.

Take a match and tear it off close to the head. Push the head into the cigarette so that the striking portion is level with the tobacco (Fig. 65, #2). Take an empty match packet and crease the cardboard lengthways. Get the cigarette into thumb palm position and lay the empty packet over it (#1). The cigarette is concealed perfectly. Pantomime the invisible match business. Bring hands to face cupped. Fold match packet over into closed position. Strike match in cigarette on phosphorus of match packet (#4). Lower hands. You have a perfect lit cigarette from nowhere and without any gimmicks!

Note: Don't inhale at this point.

The other three cigarettes are dummies. See #3 in Fig. 65.

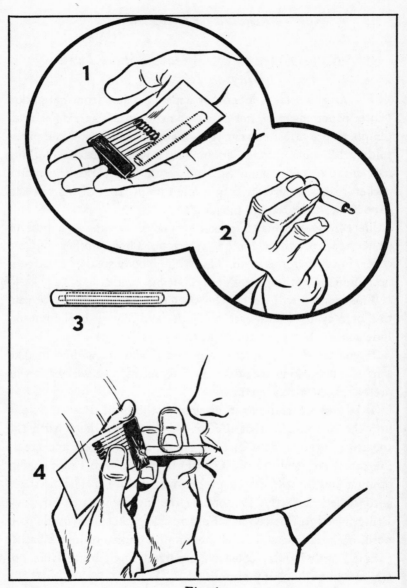

Fig. 65

Each fits within the other. They are simply rolled cardboard covered with cigarette paper. The moves work themselves. You have two cigarettes thumb palmed. One is the ordinary cigarette with the match head in it, the other, is the set of three dummies which telescope inside each other.

Proceed up to the cloud of smoke from the cigarette—now puff out a cloud of smoke, retaining some in your mouth. Reach into the smoke and produce the dummies as one. Put in mouth and puff out the stolen smoke. Now comes the beautiful move. Thumb palm the dummy and throw—the outside shell rides off into an ash tray and you are left with a dummy thumb-palmed with the lit end (red paper) in the thumb palm. Puff on real cigarette—blow smoke—hold some in mouth—produce dummy, merely revolving end for end—puff—throw and thumb palm. Puff—hold smoke—and produce the last dummy.

The nicest part of all this is that each time the dummy goes to the mouth, the magician shows his hands empty except for the lit cigarette in left hand and yet the instant the dummy is thrown away the magician has the next cigarette ready for production. I think this is a real utility device that will find its way into the routine of anyone who has ever wanted a good cigarette production.

BLOOMIN' SILK [*John P. Hamilton*]

A ping pong ball is converted into the needed prop by cutting two holes in it. One hole is ¾ of an inch in diameter, the other, opposite hole (see Fig. 66, #1) is ⅝ of an inch in diameter. Paint the ball flesh color.

A note prior to Mr. Hamilton's routine. One of the best and least used magic ball moves is shown in #2 and #3. On any occasion when a ball with a hole in it is being manipulated, you are able to do a perfect vanish with this little sequence. Assume

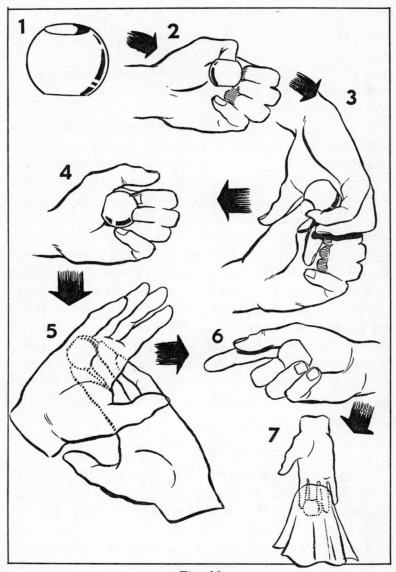

Fig. 66

you have the ball in your left hand. You have tucked a silk handkerchief into the ball (seemingly into the bare hand) with the fingers of the right hand. As the last bit of silk is tucked into the ball, insert the left thumb into the hole in the ball as in #2. Continue to pretend to tuck the silk into the hand with the forefinger of the right hand. With the forefinger of the right hand inside the left hand as in #3, lift the left thumb straight up. The ball is transferred invisibly from the left hand to the right palm. Retain it in the right palm as you gesture at the left loose fist with the right hand. Open the left hand and expose the palm. The silk has vanished.

Now, on with Hamilton's "Bloomin' Silk": Needed are the flesh colored ping pong ball with two holes cut in it, a gimmick sold by magic dealers under the name of "The Silk to Rose," a small blue silk and a red silk tucked into the ping pong ball. The gimmick for the "Silk to Rose" effect is in the handkerchief pocket of the jacket.

With the loaded ping pong ball palmed in the right hand, gesture at any blue object, like a blue flower on your table. Make a loose fist of the right hand, reach into the fist with the left fingers, and pull the blue silk into view. When the silk is almost all the way out of the ball, let go of it with the left hand and retain it with the right, displaying it with the right hand.

Hold the left hand palm outwards and draw the silk through the left hand a few times. The last time this move is made leave the ball and silk in the left hand, with the silk hiding the ball. Then form the left hand into a fist and draw the silk out with the right hand.

Use the right hand to tuck the silk back into the hidden ball in the left hand. Use the middle right finger to tuck the final bit of silk into the ball and, as you do so, bring the ball out of the left palm and hold it as in #4 on the back of the middle fingers of the left hand.

Wave the right hand in the air as though casting a magic spell (which, incidentally, lets the audience see that the right hand is empty), then bring both hands close together, making a turn to the left with the body and transferring the ball from the left hand to the right hand palm.

Open the fingers of the left hand one at a time, while pointing at the left hand with the right forefinger. At the same time the middle right finger tip enters the hole in the palmed ball between the silk and the inside of the ball.

Swing both hands shoulder high, outward, right hand behind the left with the ball on the right middle finger tip held against the back of the left as in #5. Bring both hands down, swing to the left, then to the right, palming the ball off the finger tip into the left palm and point at the right hand showing it to be empty.

Pretend to catch something in the air with the left hand, forming it into a fist. Work the blue silk from the ball with the left fingers which makes a pretty one hand production of the silk.

Secure the ball on the right middle finger tip (#6) again and you can display the silk with an obviously empty palm as in #7. Swing the ball from the finger tip into the palm and display the silk with the finger tips of both hands.

Secure the ball in the left hand and commence to tuck the silk into the top of the left fist. When it is halfway in, stop and draw the red silk from the bottom of the fist, working a color-change.

When the blue silk has completely "changed" into a red one, display the red one as in #7.

Place the red silk in the breast pocket over the "Silk to Rose" gimmick, stealing out the rose gimmick under cover of tucking the silk into the pocket, and then seemingly changing your mind and removing the silk again.

Holding the silk and the gimmick in your left hand, look at the silk questioningly, and put your right hand into your jacket pocket getting rid of the ball as you do so.

Remove the empty right hand and use it and the left hand to perform the "Silk to Rose" effect. Your hands are clean and you have an effective finish to a very pretty silk routine.

(The effect of the Silk to Rose is precisely what the title implies, a silk handkerchief visibly shapes itself into a rose bud.)

JOCKO THE GREAT [*J. G. Thompson, Jr.*]

For downright entertainment of the type that pleases any audience from grandparents to grandchildren, a hand puppet routine, cleverly presented, is difficult to surpass.

Since the appearance on the market of Hodes' Fur Monkey, there has been an increased interest shown in the finger-produced antics of the little creatures, but no real progress has been made toward the concoction of much needed new routines, of which there is a dearth in magical literature. As a matter of fact, I can't recall any. Ideas—yes, but satisfactory routines—no. So, perhaps there is room for the following, part of which is original and part of which has been adapted from other sources.

Some of Jocko the puppet's best performances have been given as a somewhat inept but always ultimately successful magician. I propose that he retain that role, but that it be elaborated upon.

The first item needed is a rectangular box, preferably with a lid that will slide off and on. This will serve two purposes: (1) As a container to hold Jocko's props and Jocko himself and (2) as a table behind which Jocko performs (Fig. 67, #1.). Actually, with the lid off and the box turned with its side open toward the rear, it looks more like a bar than anything else. It should

Fig. 67

be about 3½ inches high and approximately the same width. The length is determined largely by the space required for the props when packed for carrying, and the working space needed by the little fellow when he is performing.

On the bottom of the box paint THE GREAT JOCKO in large letters and, if so desired, you can attach a piece of felt to the side, that will serve as a table top. Each individual will have his own ideas regarding further suitable decoration which can be given the box.

Rather than list all the props, of which there are quite a few, they will be introduced as the description of the routine progress. At the beginning, most of them are under the table top, inside the box, which should be sitting on a card table near the rear edge and toward the left side.

First item on the agenda is the forcing of a card, say the 5H. Proficiency in this department is not essential. Hull's *New Idea Deck* will do nicely, as will the *Svengali* deck. A little Duke pack is also required and should be on the table with the 5H removed.

Following the introductory remarks, during which the card is forced and retained by a spectator, sit down at the left side of your table with your left side toward the audience. In this position it is natural to lean forward slightly as the puppet is operated, which permits resting your left arm on the table—a necessity you will understand later.

One more word at the outset—if you think of and talk to the puppet as though he were human throughout, practically all of your patter problems will be solved automatically and the entire performance will become a realistic one, productive of many additional laughs. In short, you will have, in effect, a "vent" routine, with the puppet acting his part in pantomime.

Introduce your little friend as "Jocko, who claims he is a

magician." He arises from behind his table, carrying a miniature wand (obtainable from many dealers), leans over and points with it to "The Great," which is facing the audience. Correct the title in your best M. C. manner, after which he bows left, center, and right.

PERFORMER. So you're a magician? (Jocko nods and pulls out a large card from his table on which is printed in big, block letters, "Second Greatest Magician In The World.")

PERFORMER. Who is the greatest? (Points to you.) He's just doing that because he wants to eat this week. Well, if you're a magician, let's see you do something.

On the table is standing a *Miniature Square Circle* (made by Merv Taylor) from which he produces a small silk (#2). During this action you may have to assist as each piece is being shown, a procedure upon which you insist. After the production, he brings out a small nickel cylinder (known as the *Presto Vanishing Tube*) and pushes the silk therein, first showing it empty to the audience and you. With the silk out of sight, he again shows the tube to you, points it toward the audience over your left arm and, as he takes it toward the table, hooks the pin attached to the inner tube to your left coat sleeve, which leaves the latter hidden behind your arm as the outer tube is carried to and set upon Jocko's table. A wave or two of the tiny wand and the vanish is disclosed.

PERFORMER. Well, that was rather good, but what are you waiting for? (He dives down and reappears with an APPLAUSE sign. As he replaces the card, he brings forth a medal, fashioned from cardboard, silk, and a small sharp hook, and pins it on his coat.)

PERFORMER. Real cocky, aren't you? (Nods and proceeds with Miniature Die Box [Lou Tannen], passing the die into your left hand. All of the sucker angles can be developed nicely because you serve as the dupe and appear surprised upon finding the die in your hand.)

At this point Jocko's attention is attracted by a pretty girl in the audience to whom he waves and whistles (if you can do the latter successfully without moving your lips). Admonish him that there must be no more of that. As you turn your head, he waves again. You catch him in the act, whereupon he pretends to be scratching his head.

PERFORMER. You are aware of the fact that a card has been chosen by a member of your audience? (Nods.) Do you think you can find it? (Nods again.) Very well, go ahead. (Replaces everything that is on the table top, inside and brings out the Little Duke playing cards and a blindfold. The latter may be made from a short length of black tape and a piece of narrow elastic. Place it around the head of Jocko, remarking that he evidently is going to do this feat the hard way. Jocko spreads the cards and finally picks one, which proves to be incorrect.)

(He tries again, attempting to see surreptitiously down along his nose by tilting his head back. Next he pushes the blindfold up a little. Scold him, whereupon he proceeds to choose an incorrect card again.)

PERFORMER. (Removing blindfold.) We might as well take this off. You're not doing well at all. (Jocko disappears and reappears with a small American flag, which he waves vigorously for sympathy and applause. Returning flag, he brings out a pair of glasses. These can be fashioned from wire and painted black, or cut from cardboard. Put them on him, after which he is unsuccessful for the third time in finding the card. Remove the glasses and set a dunce cap on his head. He cries, sobbing with his paws over his eyes.)

PERFORMER. That will get you nowhere. (He gradually stops, finally lifting one paw and looking out. Then he wipes his eyes on your handkerchief, pulling it out a bit from your breast pocket. After this, he sadly takes off the medal and puts it away. Following much deliberation, he picks out the wrong card again, whereupon in anger, he throws the cards right and left.)

PERFORMER. Stop it! We'll have none of that! (Beckons to you and, as you lean over, he whispers in your right ear.)

PERFORMER. Where do you want to go? (He brings out a card containing the words *Ladies Room.*)

PERFORMER. That's impossible. You're stalling. (Whispers again.) So what if you are nervous? (Comes up with a small liquor bottle.) You're too young for whiskey. (Brings out a tiny bottle of beer.) You can't have that either. (Meanwhile you have lighted a cigarette and he points to that.) I shouldn't let you have this, but— what have you got to trade? (Brings out cigar—gives it to you and takes cigarette, holding it up to his mouth. He starts to reel after a second or two.)

PERFORMER. You're getting sick. (Take cigarette. He grabs for your handkerchief, which he pulls from your pocket and lays on his table, upchucking into it convulsively. He finishes, rubs his face in the handkerchief and lays it on your left arm.)

PERFORMER. Not there. Put it back where you got it. (This he does, taking the tube along and dropping it in your pocket with the handkerchief which leaves you clean.)

PERFORMER. The trouble with you is that when you're learning how to do these things, you don't pay enough attention to detail. That's what counts—detail. (Hesitates a moment thoughtfully and then pulls up his tail, which he holds before you hopefully.)

PERFORMER. No, no, not that. Haven't you forgotten something? (Taps the right paw on the table top nervously and then brings out small stand [pyramidal block with concave recess at one point] and a tiny crystal ball [clear marble] which he places on the stand. After peering intently into the crystal from every conceivable angle [the more improbable the better]; and listening to your admonition to the effect that this is his *big* moment, he pulls out a large 5H [giant card]. Then he applauds madly, bowing right and left to bring his performance to a conclusion.)

If you don't get real entertainment value from this routine— then I will be very unhappy—and so will Jocko!

ESKOW'S ACT

Show your audience a piece of rope about five feet long, and a silk handkerchief. Using these two prosaic objects, a few spectators from the audience, and a borrowed dollar bill, you present ten or fifteen minutes of fast, perplexing, laughable magic.

The magician invites a spectator up on stage to help him with a problem. He has a piece of rope which must be cut exactly in two. They decide to put the two ends together and cut it right through the center, which they do.

Somehow one piece comes out about six inches longer than the other, which will never do, so the magician cuts off the excess piece, which he places in the spectator's coat pocket as a souvenir to show his grandchildren. He knots the two ropes together and hands them to his assistant to hold. He announces that his rope trick is different from anybody else's because the spectator is going to do the trick himself!

All he has to do is follow the magician's actions exactly and since he hasn't another piece of rope the magician takes out a silk handkerchief, twists it to resemble a rope and goes through a series of movements which the spectator imitates. Suddenly the magician pulls his handkerchief taut—the spectator follows suit with the rope—and the rope is in one piece! Applause for the assistant and congratulations all around. But let's not stop——

Now, announces the magician, the most amazing solid-through-solid trick ever attempted. He is going to pass the silk handkerchief through the rope without damaging either object. The spectator holds the ends of the rope while the magician ties the silk about it with two knots. Cautioning the spectator to hold the rope tightly, he declares that the handkerchief will penetrate the rope on the count of three—and nothing happens. The handkerchief is still tied to the rope, and the only one fooled is the magician—first time something like that has happened to him since '88.

Well—might as well try another trick—he can't miss all the time. So, while the spectator still holds the rope and silk, he borrows a dollar bill. He has a little difficulty doing this. Seems since his recent failure people are loath to part with their money. But he gets one and the owner comes on up too, to keep an eye on his property.

The magician rips the corner off the bill and presents the little piece to the owner to hold onto for future identification. Magician has the owner light a cigarette—to calm his nerves for one thing—and for another, declares he, the magician will cause this dollar bill to disappear, float through space and reappear in the heart of the same cigarette that the gentleman is puffing on!

He never fails twice! He folds the bill up and tosses it in the air. It has disappeared. So far, so good. Slowly and deliberately, he rolls up his sleeves and takes the burning cigarette, flicks the sparks off, breaks it in two and finds—tobacco! This is impossible. He tears all the other cigarettes in the gentleman's pack in two, frantically searching for the bill, but no greenback. Two tricks in a row, both colossal failures. Well, let's try the handkerchief and rope again.

He walks over to spectator #1 and grasps the ends of the handkerchief—one, two, three—and the cloth penetrates right through the rope! He walks over to spectator #2, who feels the knot. There is something there. The spectator unties the knot and finds the missing dollar bill, complete except for the corner which matches perfectly. Success all around and applause!

The magician is so delighted with this turn in his fortunes and so pleased with the way the spectators have helped him that he decides to show them an amazing secret, a way of making a dollar bill increase, a way of making really big money.

Just one thing he asks in return for this secret—silence, because inflation will set in immediately if this gets around.

He gives back the corner of the bill, folds the remainder in quarters and places the bill back in the owner's hands, asking the owner to squeeze tightly. He makes the magic passes and the spectator makes the magic passes. The hand is opened and it is certainly big money now! In fact, the dollar is now a foot long and six inches wide, a definite increase.

He gives the giant bill to the spectator but the corner doesn't match the giant bill and anyway, the spectator wants his own smaller but more valuable dollar back. So the magician makes the magic passes again. He says he will cause the bill to appear in a lit cigarette. No, he won't, he remembers what happened last time he tried that. So guess where he will make the bill appear—give up?

Remember that little piece of rope he gave the first spectator for a souvenir? He plucks that from the spectator's pocket, holds it up, and slowly extracts the missing dollar bill from deep down in its interior! And once again the corner matches! Applause once more. Spectator #1 takes his rope, #2 takes his bill, and the magician takes his bow. Finis.

Both the rope and the handkerchief are gimmicked in a simple and undetectable manner.

Take two dollar bills and place them one upon the other, aligning all edges exactly. With Washington staring up at you, taking care not to disarrange the alignment, rip off the top right hand corner of both bills. Each of these corners will match both bills. Discard one corner and place the other in your left hand coat pocket so it is readily accessible.

If you will look at one end of your rope you will notice that it has a core of three strands, with the outer strands wrapped about this core to make the rope as you see it. If this core is pulled while restraining the outer strands with the other hand, you can pull out the core and have nothing but a hollow tube of rope left. This principle has been used before and is the basis of the dollar bill-in-rope effect, which is a terrific climax.

Pull out about six inches of the core of your rope, cut off, and discard. You now have a hollowed-out portion in the end of your rope. One of the bills is rolled endwise into a tight tube and worked into this hollowed portion. Cut off the remainder of the hollow, leaving just enough to cover the end of the bill. You now have a piece of rope which looks perfectly ordinary—and you are all set for the last trick. Bend the bill a bit, after it is inside the rope, to remove its stiffness and you are all set to do the rope trick.

Spread your silk handkerchief out on the table. Fold the second bill into quarters and in half again. Place a tiny dab of wax on the bill and stick it firmly to the center of the silk. Fold the silk so that when you unfold it, the dollar bill will be on the side toward you, and then place it in any convenient pocket. Your set-up is almost complete. Fold a giant fake bill until it is approximately the size of a real bill folded in quarters and place it in your right hand pocket.

Exhibit rope freely, holding ungimmicked side in left hand. Get spectator and give him the scissors. Place both ends of the rope in your left hand and execute the standard rope move, which permits the rope apparently to be cut in two. Actually, a small loop of rope is cut, simulating the two cut ends.

When the ends of the rope are dropped, one end will be about six inches longer than the other. This is the end containing the bill. You must now even up the ends. Grasp the longer end to mark off how much must be cut. Then have the spectator cut this piece off. Ropes are now even and you are holding the end containing the bill. Casually thrust this end into the spectator's breast pocket, making some remark about "souvenirs," and leave it there. By the time you get around to it again everyone has forgotten its existence—and the revelation of the bill becomes even more mysterious when they realize the rope has never left the spectator's pocket.

To return to the two pieces of rope. They are knotted together as follows: Twist a loop into the right hand piece of rope. Place this loop over the two ends projecting from your hand and pull tight. Actually, you are tying an overhand knot which covers the juncture between the little segment of rope and the big piece.

Now take the scissors and start trimming down your ends above the knot. On your last cut, the scissors grasp the half inch or so of rope end still left in the knot and pull out. The little pieces go to the floor and, though your rope still has a knot in its center, it is now in one piece. Give the rope to the spectator to hold by one end. Now you want to teach him how to restore it. Grope in your pocket for another piece of rope. You don't have one. Come out with the handkerchief which you will use instead. Hold by two corners and allow to unfold. Bill is toward you and unseen by the spectator.

Fold two edges, bringing them together so the bill goes inside, and rope up the handkerchief. There is no need to call attention to the silk. It's just being used for demonstrating anyway. Now you have a roped silk with a dollar bill inside. You do a few little actions with the silk which the spectator imitates. Touch the ends together three times, say the magic words and put the two ends to your ears. Spectator follows suit. Now direct all eyes to the rope. The trick is about to begin. Snap your hands apart. The spectator does the same, pulling out the knot, and the rope melts into one piece in his hand!

He takes a bow and your audience will applaud. Build up

your great penetration trick and proceed as follows. Spectator holds the rope horizontally, one end in each hand. Proceed to tie the rope around the silk in the following manner. The first knot is the well known vanishing knot. Follow the moves in Fig. 68, #1-2-3-4-5-6, which explain it completely. The right end is then brought over and under as shown and a regular overhand knot is tied. If the ends of the handkerchief are pulled, it will pass right through the rope, leaving one knot still in the silk. That's what you say you are going to do, but you don't, not yet. "One, two, three . . ." And nothing happens—since you don't pull. The silk remains knotted around the rope. The dollar bill is in the center of the knot. And another bill is still in that little piece of rope . . .

"We'll try something else . . ." As you patter and ask for a dollar bill, your left hand casually goes to the left pocket and finger-palms the corner. The donor gives you the bill which you take in the left hand, the corner going underneath. The right hand removes the right hand corner of the bill openly. You start to give the bill back but then decide to give the corner back instead. The left hand moves the bill over to the right. The right hand places the real corner on top of the bill and grasps the bill. The left hand comes away and shows the duplicate corner which is given to the owner. Apparently the bill is put from the left hand into the right and the corner taken in the left. The switch is absolutely clean, subtle, and undetectable.

Have the spectator light up a cigarette while you fold the bill into quarters. The real corner is folded up inside. You may now dispose of the bill in your favorite manner. I simply palm it when I pretend to place it in my other hand, but you may prefer to use the slit envelope so that you can apparently burn the bill.

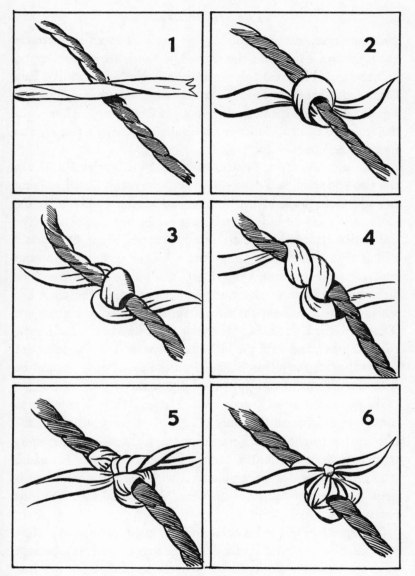

Fig. 68

At any rate, the bill vanishes and the announcement is made about finding it in the lit cigarette. The hands are shown empty, and the bill is impressively torn in half. Nothing—and be flabbergasted when you fail! Take the pack and tear up all the cigarettes in the gentleman's pack. Still nothing. After your discomfiture and two failures have gathered enough laughs, you now proceed to turn the tables.

Return to the spectator who still has the rope and silk. Grasp the two ends and pull—the silk penetrates visibly! Still holding the silk aloft, walk back to the second spectator. He feels the knot—and feels his bill. He unties the knot himself, extracts the bill and matches the corner. If you stopped right here you'd still have a great trick! Drape the silk over your left arm and wait for your applause (you'll get it, too) to die down. Your right hand goes into your right pocket and steals the giant bill while you patter about showing them how to make big money. Take back the bill, placing it in your right hand over the finger-palmed giant, and fold the bill into quarters. Tell the spectator you will place the bill in his hand on the count of three and he is to close his hand tightly when he gets it.

As you count slowly, your hand is raised on each number as though to emphasize the count. The right thumb pulls back the bill and the right fingers push out the giant so that the spectator gets the giant on the count of three. He closes his hand. You pick up the silk from your arm with the right hand and it goes into your pocket, thus disposing of the real bill. The rest is easy.

The spectator opens his hand and the giant is displayed. Now you can afford to build up the last appearance of the bill because you're completely through. Pull the little piece from the first spectator's pocket. Show your hands completely empty and slowly force the bill out of the rope. When it is about halfway out, have the spectator remove it completely. He unrolls it and matches the corner once more, to the complete mystification of your audience. Give back the *souvenir*, and offer a new pack of cigarettes for the one you destroyed, dismiss your assistants, and *bow*.

The Last Word

And so we come to an end. I hope you have enjoyed the more than one hundred tricks that I have described. I know there is something here for every performer, rank amateur or slick professional, because in all this wealth of material, some of the finest of the contributions of my many friends in the world of magic, there is some of the best magic extant today.

I hope the beginner, coming to this fascinating world for the first time, will be as enchanted by magic as I, and I sincerely hope that the informed amateur will have learned some new tricks that he will enjoy.

As always, I want to extend my heartfelt thanks to my friends for permission to print their cherished secrets. I hope I have done them justice.

INDEX

Index